*Football Food*

UNIVERSITY PRESS OF FLORIDA

Florida A&M University, Tallahassee
Florida Atlantic University, Boca Raton
Florida Gulf Coast University, Ft. Myers
Florida International University, Miami
Florida State University, Tallahassee
New College of Florida, Sarasota
University of Central Florida, Orlando
University of Florida, Gainesville
University of North Florida, Jacksonville
University of South Florida, Tampa
University of West Florida, Pensacola

Kellie Lawless and Maili Brocke

GAINESVILLE · TALLAHASSEE · TAMPA

JACKSONVILLE · FT. MYERS · SARASOTA

BOCA RATON · PENSACOLA · ORLANDO · MIAMI

UNIVERSITY PRESS OF FLORIDA

# FOOTBALL

## Food

13   12   11   10   09   08   6   5   4   3   2   1

A record of cataloging-in-publication data is available from the
Library of Congress.
ISBN 978-0-8130-3244-3

The University Press of Florida is the scholarly publishing agency
for the State University System of Florida, comprising Florida
A&M University, Florida Atlantic University, Florida Gulf Coast
University, Florida International University, Florida State University,
New College of Florida, University of Central Florida, University of
Florida, University of North Florida, University of South Florida,
and University of West Florida.

University Press of Florida
15 Northwest 15th Street
Gainesville, FL 32611-2079
http://www.upf.com

To my mother, who had the good sense to move us to San Francisco just in time for the glory years. I love you.

*Kellie*

To all the football players in my life, who like to eat almost as much as they like to play the game.

*Maili*

# Contents

*Acknowledgments  ix*
*Are You Ready for Some Football Food?  xi*

It All Started in New Jersey  1

Finger Food and Nibbles: Kick-Off Fare  4

The Least You Need to Know—Gridiron Basics  28

Gridiron Grilling: Tailgate and Backyard BBQ Favorites  33

Tips on Tailgating  52

Sandwiches: Hearty Handfuls  55

Any Given Sunday: Morning Specials for Early Games  67

Halftime Extravaganzas: Main Dishes for the Hungriest Fans  80

Bowl Food: Soups, Stews, and Chilis  98

Sideline Players: Beans to Breads, Pasta to Potatoes  114

End Zone Celebrations: Our Best Sweet Conclusions  133

Surviving the Off-Season  154

Beyond Beer: Sure-Fire Thirst Quenchers  157

Team Efforts: Menus for Every Setting  171

*Index  197*

# Acknowledgments

Overwhelming gratitude to our agent, Stephany, who found the perfect home for this book, sustaining a few late hits in the process. We'll make a football fan out of you yet!

Boundless love to Lissa Young, who talked Kellie through the great state of Virginia and, somewhere around Roanoke, made a suggestion that would change the destiny of this book. Thank you for bringing us together.

Heartfelt appreciation to Diana LaSalle, who provided sage advice, unwavering faith, and unrelenting self-sacrifice in the pursuit of the perfect fish taco recipe.

Special thanks to Stephen Potter, who was kind enough to share his expertise so that we could explain the fundamentals of the game.

Cheers to Ray Daniels, Craft Beer marketing director for the Brewers Association, who provided an outstanding list of regional beers.

Enthusiastic kudos to the team of recipe testers who gave of their time and their grocery budget to help us perfect these dishes.

Special appreciation to all the wonderful participants on Maili's recipe testing e-mail list, who provided priceless feedback, knowledge, and information—thanks for letting me flood your inboxes; to Ann Hutchison and Karen Williams, who have unfailingly been by my side through every recipe; to my family, friends, and neighbors who came by to eat the results; and to my husband, who loves to eat more than anyone I know.

True admiration for the cast of characters, on and off the field, who make the game what it is.

# Are You Ready for Some Football Food?

For most of us, it starts out innocently enough. Wanting to spend time with dad, you pull up a seat and catch the Saturday game while he watches his favorite team and questions the eyesight of the referees. You go off to college and the fall social scene revolves around Homecoming and tailgate parties. You graduate, join the work force, and find yourself reliving highlights from Monday night games with coworkers on Tuesday morning. The next thing you know, you're celebrating the first Sunday in February as though it were a national holiday. You're a full-blown football fan. That's how it happened for us, anyway.

Football is more than something we watch on television or from stadium seats. It's something we experience—an integral part of our lives and a passion we share with others. The American Tailgaters Association estimates that more than 20 million people pull into a parking lot each year to enjoy pre-game festivities, and Super Bowl Sunday is now a de facto national holiday, with nearly a *billion* people watching the game worldwide! Whether you're a weekend warrior who catches a Sunday game, a crazed alumni with season tickets, a *Monday Night Football* fanatic, or among the millions who tune in to watch The Game the first weekend in February, football is more fun when you share it with friends, family, and some traditional football fare.

That's why we created *Football Food*, a collection of recipes, fun facts, and stories that celebrate the game and its followers. It's filled with classic, easy comfort food with a few updated and delicious twists. From traditional choices like Buffalo Wings, Guacamole, and Beer Can Chicken to our family favorites like Pork Picadillo and Cider-Stewed Chicken, these are the recipes we reach for when friends and family con-verge.

Whether you're a fan yourself or just enjoy the gather-ings, everything in the book is designed to work around the gridiron action with a maximum of advance preparation and a minimum of fuss during game time. We've even included notes in the recipes to help you plan the meal around half-time and commercial breaks. There's nothing worse than be-ing stuck in the kitchen when shouts emerge from the living room—"Oh man! I can't *believe* he caught that pass!" These recipes guarantee that you'll be there to see it too. And for stress-free football party planning, we have included a whole chapter on menus that give you a game plan guaranteed to please no matter what the score.

If you're one of the millions who love tailgating, we've noted recipes that travel well and get rave reviews at the sta-dium. Check out Tips on Tailgating for some fresh ideas for parking lot feasts.

*Football Food* has been a labor of love for both of us. May you enjoy the recipes, and may your team make it to the championship game!

# It All Started in New Jersey

The origins of football date back to the 1820s, when students at Princeton started playing a game called "ballown." The goal was to use the player's fist to advance the ball past the opposing team. It wasn't long before Harvard students joined the action, playing pick-up games on Boston Common. It would be another 40 years before a rudimentary version of modern-day football emerged, but by that time, the game had become so popular that colleges began organizing intercollegiate games.

In 1920 football turned pro. First called the American Professional Football League, two years later it was given the name by which we know it today—the National Football League (NFL). While college football enjoyed a strong regional fan base, professional football teams struggled financially and seemed unable to tap into the passion Americans had for baseball. All that would change on December 28, 1958.

On that day, 45 million Americans tuned in for the first televised football game: the NFL championship between the league's dominant franchise, the New York Giants, and the young, brash Baltimore Colts. With a minute and 45 seconds remaining in the game, and the Giants leading 17–14, 25-year-old quarterback Johnny Unitas trotted into the huddle, peered stoically at his teammates, and declared, "We've got 86 yards and two minutes. Let's get to work." Using every last second, Unitas guided the Colts downfield, expertly positioning the team for a 3-point field goal to tie the game.

Exhausted and bewildered, Giants place kicker Pat Summerall turned to Kyle Rote and asked, "What happens now?"

Rote replied, "I think we play some more." While it's true the NFL had instituted a rule in 1947 allowing sudden death overtime in the event of a playoff-game tie, it had never happened before—this was a first.

With the Giants forced to punt on the first drive, Unitas systematically moved the ball down to the Giants' 8-yard line—bringing 20,000 screaming Baltimore fans to their feet. And then things got interesting. The television audience, glued to their sets, suddenly saw: "Please Stand By. Picture Transmission Has Been Temporarily Interrupted." The exuberant Baltimore fans had rocked the bleachers so violently that they disconnected a television feed cable.

Unitas—unaware of the television blackout—headed into the huddle. Suddenly a drunken fan ran out onto the field and led police on a merry chase for several minutes. He was captured just as the broadcast cable was reconnected, and millions of viewers tuned in to see him handcuffed and hauled off the field. It would be years before anyone outside NBC knew that the "inebriated fan" was in fact an NBC executive desperate to buy time so that the television audience wouldn't miss the cliffhanger. Two skillfully executed plays later, the upstart Baltimore Colts won the game 23–17, and America was officially hooked on football.

Over the next decade the game would capture not only the imagination and hearts of the people but the attention of a group of wealthy businessmen. Joining together to form the American Football League, they established franchises in Boston, Dallas, Denver, Los Angeles, New York, Houston, Minneapolis, and Buffalo to compete with the NFL for ticket sales and television rights. In 1967 the two leagues merged, forming the AFC and NFC divisions under the umbrella of the NFL.

This combination of two divisions under one league proved to be pure genius. Driven by bitter rivalry not only among teams during the season but also between divisions at season's end, excited fans have turned the Super Bowl into the most watched event in broadcast history. At last estimate, the Super Bowl audience reached the billion viewer mark worldwide. And to think . . . it all started in New Jersey.

# Finger Food and Nibbles

## Kick-Off Fare

Football started gaining popularity on college campuses in the late 1800s, but at the time, it more closely resembled rugby than the game we know today. The forward pass was illegal, late hits were considered good form, and the best way to advance the ball was to push the ball carrier forcefully into the opposing line and throw a few punches at anyone who got in the way. None of this would have elicited a flag on the play!

In the early days of professional football, team members played both offensive and defensive positions. When one team lost possession of the ball, the quarterback stayed on the field, set up on the line of scrimmage, and became a defensive lineman. It was a tough game played by hardy men like Bronco Nagurski, Red Grange, and the legendary Jim Thorpe.

With players wearing little or no padding and helmets fashioned of soft leather, broken bones, concussions, and even death were not uncommon. The face guard would not be introduced for decades, and few players retired from the sport with their original teeth and nose cartilage intact.

We like our finger food to work just as hard as these early pioneers of the game, so we've chosen recipes that can be prepared in advance and placed in strategic locations for easy access. For playoff-game parties, try a succession of nibblers served throughout the game followed by a few dessert options to finish out the fourth quarter. This keeps the crowd happy, and the cook can handle food preparations during commercial breaks. Many of these dishes can also be baked in advance and gently reheated during the pregame show.

For no-fuss football entertaining, offer a couple of chilled dips that can be made a day in advance, interspersed with a hot dish or two—that way you're not in the kitchen when it's third and 10 and the quarterback drops back for a Hail Mary pass.

This classic dipping sauce is the perfect complement to cold shrimp—an easy finger food to snack on during the first quarter. It works well with cold crab too, if your team is in the playoffs and you decide to splurge.

## Classic Shrimp Cocktail Sauce

½ cup Heinz chili sauce
½ cup ketchup
1 teaspoon Pickapeppa sauce (or Worcestershire)
1 teaspoon freshly squeezed lemon juice
1 teaspoon horseradish, or more to taste
1 teaspoon brown sugar (or substitute granulated sugar)

∗

Mix all ingredients together in a bowl until sugar is dissolved. Keep refrigerated until ready to use.

*Makes 1 cup of sauce.*

The worst loss in NFL history was sustained by the Washington Redskins at the hands of the Chicago Bears. After an earlier game in the season when the Redskins boasted of their easy victory over the Bears, the stage was set for revenge. The Bears were ready and proceeded to annihilate the Redskins 73–0. At one point an official had to ask Chicago to stop kicking extra points because they were running out of footballs!

This is the hardest-working sauce in the book. It's a great dipping sauce for chilled shrimp and also goes with grilled salmon, chicken, or pork. Maili first learned about Mae Ploy Sweet Chili Sauce from army friend Teri Buzzard, who was stationed in Thailand with her parents. Previously, the sauce was available only in specialty markets, but it's now widely available in major grocery stores throughout the United States.

# Triple Citrus Thai Chili Sauce

½ cup Mae Ploy Sweet Chili Sauce (or your favorite sweet
   chili sauce)
Juice of ½ a lime (1 tablespoon juice)
Juice of ½ a lemon (1 tablespoon juice)
Juice of ½ an orange (4 tablespoons juice)
1 tablespoon sugar (can use brown or granulated sugar)
1 tablespoon fresh ginger, minced
1 tablespoon fresh cilantro, chopped

   *

Mix all ingredients together in a medium bowl until sugar is dissolved. Keep refrigerated until ready to use.

*This makes about ¾ of a cup of sauce and can be kept in the refrigerator for up to 3 weeks.*

This is the easiest recipe you'll ever make. It's a favorite at Maili's Super Bowl parties and goes well with many things, including beef, chicken, or fish tacos.

---

# Salsa Cream Sauce

1 cup of your favorite salsa
½ cup sour cream

*

Blend together in a medium bowl.

*Makes 1½ cups.*

> "The spirit, the will to win, and the will to excel are the things that endure. These qualities are so much more important than the events that occur."
>
> Vince Lombardi

This first quarter classic is quick and easy to make. The secret is keeping an avocado pit in the dip until you're ready to serve it. This prevents the avocados from turning brown.

# Goal Line Guacamole

6 ripe Haas avocados
3 teaspoons freshly squeezed lemon or lime juice
1 teaspoon kosher salt
2 tablespoons salsa

\*

Halve the avocados and remove the pits and skin, saving one pit. Squeeze lemon juice over the avocados and mash with a fork until you get the texture you want. Add kosher salt and 2 tablespoons of your favorite salsa.

This dish must be prepared the same day you plan to serve it. If you prepare it in the morning, be sure to keep the pit in the guacamole, then press plastic wrap directly against the guacamole so that it's not exposed to air. Put an additional lid or plastic wrap on the container until ready to serve with your favorite tortilla chips.

*Serves 8 to 10.*

> **"No other single American event impacts the sale of avocados like the Super Bowl."**
>
> Mark Affleck, president, California Avocado Commission

No matter what else is served at our parties, this always gets devoured first. Make sure you have copies of the recipe ready, because everyone will ask for it!

---

## Melissa's Artichoke Dip

2 14-ounce cans artichoke hearts, packed in water
    (approximately 7 hearts)
2 cups freshly shredded Parmesan cheese (powdered or
    pregrated cheeses do not work as well)
1½ cups mayonnaise
1 4-ounce can diced jalapeños
1 4-ounce can diced green chiles
Tortilla chips

\*

Preheat oven to 375º.

Drain artichokes and chop roughly. If you use artichokes packed in oil, rinse them well. Place chopped artichokes, Parmesan cheese, mayonnaise, jalapeños, and green chiles in a bowl and mix well.

Pour into a 9 × 13-inch casserole or baking dish of your choice. Cover with foil and bake for 20 minutes. Uncover and bake an additional 10 minutes until bubbly and golden. Remove from oven and serve immediately with tortilla chips.

*Makes about 6 cups.*

> The Red Zone is so called because the offense has the ball deep inside enemy territory, and the defense is on red alert for an imminent score. It is the 20 yards abutting the end zone.

Layered with flavors and textures, this Mexican-inspired dip is great when you've got a crowd. Assemble it the night before the game, then just fill a large basket with yellow and blue tortilla chips to accompany the dip.

# Red Zone Layered Dip

1 pound chorizo sausage, removed from the casing
1 small onion, chopped
1 teaspoon ancho chili powder
1 16-ounce can refried beans
1 cup sour cream
½ pound Monterey Jack cheese, grated
1 cup guacamole
1 cup salsa
⅓ cup chopped cilantro
3 green onions (white and green parts), chopped
1 2.25-ounce can sliced olives
Yellow and blue tortilla chips

*

In a medium skillet, sauté the chorizo, onion, and chili powder over medium heat for 10 minutes or until the sausage is browned. Drain and cool.

In a large bowl, combine the cooled chorizo with the refried beans. Spread the mixture on the bottom of a 9 × 13-inch glass baking dish or decorative serving dish. Spread the sour cream over the bean mixture.

Sprinkle the cheese over the top and then evenly spread with the guacamole. Top with the salsa and scatter the cilantro, green onions, and olives on top.

The dip can be covered and refrigerated or served immediately. Serve with tortilla chips.

*Serves 8 to 10.*

This is an easy dip to make in advance of the pregame show and works well with baked pita bread triangles or chips. If you're lucky enough to have some left over, use it as a sandwich spread.

# Roasted Red Pepper Dip

1 4-ounce jar roasted red peppers, with juice
1 3-ounce package cream cheese
¾ teaspoon salt
1 tablespoon parsley
2 green onions (white part only)
1 clove garlic, chopped
Pinch of cayenne pepper
1 cup sour cream

\*

In a blender, combine the roasted red peppers, cream cheese, salt, parsley, green onions, garlic, and cayenne pepper and process until smooth.

Pour the mixture into a medium bowl and stir in the sour cream.

This can be made up to two days ahead and kept in the refrigerator in an airtight container.

*Makes 2 cups.*

The longest field goal was recorded by Tom Dempsey in 1970. With only seconds to play, and the Saints trailing the Lions, Dempsey kicked a 63-yard field goal to win the game. What's most amazing is that Dempsey was born missing his right hand and part of his right foot—the one that set the record.

Dips are a cook's best friend for game day parties because they can be made days in advance and can sit in the refrigerator until the pregame show. Our Fearsome Threesome can be served with chips or a fresh vegetable tray or even seafood.

# The Fearsome Threesome

## Smoky Chip Dip

½ cup mayonnaise
½ cup sour cream
¼ teaspoon hot mustard
1 garlic clove, finely minced
1 tablespoon white wine vinegar
1 teaspoon liquid smoke
Dash cayenne pepper

\*

Combine all ingredients in a medium bowl and mix well. Chill the sauce for at least 1 hour. Serve with chips, chilled shrimp or crab legs.

*Makes 1 cup.*

## Carmelized Onion Dip

1 jumbo yellow onion or 2 medium yellow onions, cut in ¼-inch slices
2 tablespoons olive oil
½ teaspoon salt
2 cups sour cream
2 tablespoons balsamic vinegar
2 teaspoons Pickapeppa sauce (or Worcestershire)
½ teaspoon salt
1 teaspoon freshly ground pepper
4 green onions, thinly sliced (both white and green parts)
1 teaspoon of your favorite hot sauce, or more to taste

\*

Preheat the oven to 350°.

Toss onions in olive oil and salt. Line a cookie sheet with parchment paper and make an even layer of onions. Bake for 40 to 50 minutes until edges are browned. Begin checking onions after 30 minutes. The longer you cook them without burning them, the better the flavor. If they begin to brown, add ¼ cup water to the pan.

Chop the cooked onions and place in a bowl. Add sour cream, balsamic vinegar, Pickapeppa sauce, salt, ground pepper, green onions, and hot sauce. Mix until combined.

*Makes about 2½ cups.*

## Clam Dip

1 8-ounce package cream cheese, softened
1 6.5-ounce can minced clams, drained, broth reserved
1 teaspoon Worcestershire sauce

✻

In a medium bowl, combine the cream cheese, drained clams, and Worcestershire sauce. Add 4 to 6 tablespoons of the reserved broth until you get the desired consistency.

Serve immediately or cover and chill in the refrigerator. Bring to room temperature before serving. Serve with corn or potato chips.

*Makes 1 cup.*

> Linebacker Matt Millen is the only player to earn Super Bowl rings from three different teams. He played for the Los Angeles Raiders in Super Bowls XV and XVIII, the San Francisco 49ers in Super Bowl XXIV, and the Washington Redskins in Super Bowl XXVI. Millen retired after the 1991 season.

The perfect savory bite during pregame cocktail hour, these cheese crisps can be made well in advance and kept in an airtight container. You can also wrap the dough in plastic and keep it in the refrigerator for up to a week or in the freezer for up to 3 months.

# Coin Toss Cheese Crisps

1 stick (8 tablespoons) unsalted butter
2 cups (8 ounces) extra sharp cheddar cheese, grated
1 cup unbleached flour
½ teaspoon salt
½ teaspoon cayenne pepper
½ teaspoon Coleman's dry mustard, optional
¼ cup roasted pecans, chopped, optional

*

Place butter in a large mixing bowl and cream until pale yellow. Add the cheese and mix well.

In a separate bowl, combine the flour, salt, cayenne pepper, dry mustard, and roasted pecans. Gradually add flour mixture to the cheese mixture. It will be fairly stiff and hard to mix. Stir until just combined.

Put dough on wax paper and roll into logs 1" in diameter. Wrap the logs with plastic wrap and refrigerate for at least 2 hours, or until they are firm and hard. You can also freeze them for up to 3 months.

Preheat oven to 375°. Slice the logs into rounds that are ⅛" to ¼" thick. Place the rounds on a cookie sheet lined with parchment paper.

Bake about 12 minutes, or until they turn golden. Transfer to a wire cooling rack. They will stay crisp for two or three days in an airtight container.

*Makes about 5 dozen crisps.*

This simple Deviled Egg recipe is from Maili's family and goes back for generations. They are devoured so quickly that they never even make it to the table. This basic recipe can be adapted to personal taste by adding herbs, seasoning salt, flavored mustards, etc.

# First Round Draft Deviled Eggs

1 dozen eggs
1 tablespoon vinegar
⅓ cup Hellmann's Best Foods Mayonnaise
2 teaspoons mustard
⅛ teaspoon salt
Freshly ground pepper to taste
Paprika to sprinkle on eggs, optional
Parsley for garnish, optional

*

Place the eggs in a pot of cold water. Over medium-high heat, bring the water to a boil. Turn off the heat and cover the pan with a lid.

Set a timer and let the eggs sit in the water for 15 minutes. Remove the eggs and immediately rinse with cold water to stop the cooking process and avoid overcooking.

Peel the eggs and cut in half lengthwise. Carefully remove the yolks and place in a mixing bowl. Set the eggs whites on a plate or tray.

With a fork, combine the yolks with the mayonnaise, mustard, salt, and pepper and mix well. If desired, add herbs and other seasonings to taste. Carefully spoon the yolk mixture into the egg white shell and garnish with paprika and/or parsley if you wish.

*Makes 24 egg halves.*

When serving nachos, the sky's the limit for toppings and flavors. Use this recipe simply as a guide, and experiment to your heart's content. Kellie adds a teaspoon of adobo sauce to the sour cream, giving the nachos a smoky flavor. Maili piles on guacamole and pulled pork!

---

# Our Favorite Nachos

1 15-ounce can refried beans
1 cup of your favorite chunky salsa (medium or hot)
2–3 tablespoons canned jalapeños, chopped
1 small can pitted black olives, chopped
1 tomato, seeded and chopped
2 cups cheddar cheese, grated
1 large bag tortilla chips
½ cup sour cream, optional
1 teaspoon adobo sauce, optional

*

Preheat the oven to 350°. Line a large baking sheet with aluminum foil or parchment paper. Place a wire baking rack on top of the foil.

In a medium bowl, combine the beans, salsa, and canned jalapeños. (If you use fresh jalapeños, reduce the quantity to 1 tablespoon.)

Arrange the tortilla chips on the wire baking rack and drop the bean mixture, by large tablespoons, over the chips. Sprinkle with the olives and tomatoes and top with the grated cheese. Bake for 10 minutes or until the cheese is completely melted.

Using a large spatula, carefully transfer the nachos to a serving platter. Drop teaspoons of sour cream over the nachos before serving, if desired.

*Serves 8 to 10.*

These addictive nibbles can be made a week in advance and kept in an airtight container, which makes them a fuss-free favorite. They're great with cocktails before the *Monday Night Football* game.

## Spicy Cocktail Nuts

1 teaspoon salt
½ teaspoon chili powder
1 teaspoon ground cumin, optional
1 teaspoon ground cinnamon
1 teaspoon ground ginger
1 egg white
1 cup pecans
1 cup cashews
1 cup walnuts
¼ cup granulated sugar

\*

Preheat the oven to 225° and position the rack in the center. Line a baking sheet with parchment paper.

In a medium bowl, combine the salt, chili powder, optional cumin, cinnamon, and ginger.

In a large bowl, whisk the egg white until foamy, add the spice mixture, and whisk to combine. Add the pecans, cashews, and walnuts to the spice mixture and toss. Add the sugar and stir until well-coated.

Spread the nuts in a single layer on the prepared pan. Bake for 1½ hours or until the nuts are toasted, stirring occasionally. Transfer the nuts to a bowl and cool completely.

*Makes 3 cups.*

During a practice in 1989, Redskins receiver Gerald Riggs dropped back to receive a pass and collided with a pickup truck parked near the sidelines. Luckily, Riggs was completely unhurt. The truck was not as fortunate, sustaining $1,370 worth of damage, including a severely dented door and a broken window.

Every self-respecting sports bar has a version of this football food classic. Our recipe was developed for a friend whose doctor ordered her off fried foods. By baking the wings, we also avoid last minute fussing with the fryer and loss of game watching time. Paper napkins are not a luxury with this dish!

# Baked Buffalo Wings

4 pounds chicken wingettes (or use wings and separate the parts before baking)
6 tablespoons canola oil
2 cloves garlic, minced
1 teaspoon salt
1¼ teaspoons cayenne pepper
4 teaspoons apple cider vinegar
¼ cup chili sauce
1 tablespoon hot chili sauce or hot sauce
⅔ cup mayonnaise
⅓ cup sour cream
1 cup blue cheese, crumbled
Salt and pepper to taste
10 celery ribs, cut into sticks

*

Preheat the oven to 425°. Line a large baking sheet with aluminum foil. Place a baking rack on top of the foil.

In a large bowl, combine the oil, garlic, salt, and cayenne. Add the chicken wingettes and coat them completely with the oil mixture. Place the coated wings in a single layer on the baking rack and bake about 30 minutes or until chicken is golden brown.

In a non-reactive bowl, combine the mayonnaise, sour cream, blue cheese, salt, and pepper and refrigerate until needed.

In a large bowl, combine the vinegar, chili sauce, and hot chili sauce. When the wings come out of the oven, add them to the bowl and toss to coat.

Serve the wings on a platter with the blue cheese dip and celery sticks alongside. They're messy, so be sure to have lots of paper napkins on hand.

*Serves 8 to 10.*

The "All-Madden" Team is an unofficial all-star team compiled each year by former Oakland Raiders coach and TV football broadcaster John Madden. Each year he names his favorite players to the team. For a player to be selected, Madden must have seen him play in person that year, and he must embody the qualities that Madden believes make a great football player: grit, determination, and a willingness to get dirty. It is considered a great honor to be named to the team.

Like all great finger food, this playoff game favorite is messy. Make sure you have plenty of napkins on hand or a large dog with a taste for barbecue. The sauce can be made a day or two in advance and stored in the refrigerator.

# Barbecue Cocktail Riblets

1 tablespoon vegetable oil
1 small onion
1 clove garlic, minced
⅔ cup bourbon
⅔ cup chili sauce
½ cup apple cider vinegar
3 tablespoons honey
½ teaspoon ground ginger
3 tablespoons plum jam
5 pounds baby back ribs (have the butcher cut them into
   3" lengths)
Salt and pepper to taste

\*

Heat the oil in a large saucepan. Add the onions and sauté them for about 10 minutes or until they are soft but not brown. Add the remaining sauce ingredients and bring to a simmer, stirring occasionally. Reduce the heat to low and cook until the mixture thickens, about 35 minutes; allow to cool.

Season the ribs with salt and pepper and place them in a large resealable plastic bag. Pour the barbecue sauce over the ribs and allow them to marinate in the refrigerator for at least 4 hours or overnight.

Preheat the oven to 375°. Line a baking sheet with aluminum foil and put a baking rack on top of the foil. Remove the ribs from the marinade and place on top of the baking rack.

Roast the ribs for 40 to 55 minutes or until the ribs are crispy on the outside and tender to the bone. Serve the ribs immediately on a large serving platter or tray.

*Serves 4 to 6.*

Potato skins are always a crowd pleaser, and you can add just about any topping you want. The potatoes can be baked a day in advance to save time on game day. Just load 'em up and run them under the broiler before kick-off.

## Classic Potato Skins

4 large russet potatoes
3 tablespoons olive oil
Salt to taste
½ cup grated cheddar cheese
3 green onions (including 1" of the green), chopped
4 slices bacon, cooked and crumbled
½ cup sour cream

*

Preheat the oven to 400°.

Scrub the potatoes and prick with a fork. Bake for 45 minutes or until soft when pierced with a knife. Cool the potatoes until they can be handled.

Cut the potatoes in half lengthwise and scoop out the flesh. Be careful to leave ¼" of potato on the skin. Halve the potatoes again lengthwise and place them on a baking sheet.

Preheat the broiler. Brush the skins with the olive oil and sprinkle with salt. Place under the broiler for about 5 to 6 minutes or until lightly browned.

Remove the skins from the broiler and fill them with the cheese, scallions, and bacon. Run the skins back under the broiler until the cheese melts. Serve the skins on a platter, dotted with sour cream.

*Makes 16 potato skins.*

This recipe makes 24 individual pieces, so it's our "go to" recipe for game crowds. Wingettes can be substituted for the drumettes and are often easier to find at the grocery store.

# Honey Mustard Chicken Drumettes

24 chicken drumettes or wingettes (or use whole wings)
Salt to taste
⅓ cup canola oil
⅓ cup honey
¼ cup tamari sauce (soy sauce can be substituted)
¼ cup Dijon mustard
¼ cup lemon juice
2 cloves garlic, minced

✳

Sprinkle the drumettes with salt. Place the chicken in a large resealable plastic bag.

In a medium bowl, combine the oil, honey, tamari sauce, mustard, lemon juice, and garlic. Pour the marinade over the chicken and refrigerate for at least 3 hours or overnight, turning occasionally.

Preheat the oven to 400°. Line a large baking sheet with aluminum foil. Place a wire rack on the baking sheet. Place the drumettes or wingettes on the rack, reserving the marinade.

Bake for 20 minutes, then remove from oven, turn the chicken, and baste with reserved marinade. Return chicken to oven and bake an additional 25 minutes, or until golden brown and glossy. Serve immediately. Alternatively, cool the chicken, refrigerate and gently reheat in a 325° oven for 15 minutes.

*Makes 24 pieces.*

Kellie's mom has served this salsa for *Monday Night Football* gatherings from coast to coast. It's easy to make and appealing to all ages. Serve with an assortment of tortilla chips.

---

# Black Bean Salsa

2 cups of your favorite salsa
1 15-ounce can black beans, partially drained
1–2 green onions, chopped
1 avocado, chopped
1 teaspoon ground cumin, optional
1 tablespoon fresh cilantro, chopped

Combine all the ingredients in a medium bowl.

Let stand at room temperature, covered, for 30 minutes before serving.

*Makes about 4 cups of salsa.*

After giving this dish a try, you may never buy premade salsa again! It's quick and easy to make, yet still tastes like you used fresh tomatoes from your garden. No chopping, seeding, peeling—just great salsa in seconds.

# No-Chop Salsa

2½ tablespoons canned diced jalapeños
¼ small onion, cut in four pieces
2 cloves garlic
1 28-ounce can diced tomatoes
2 tablespoons lime juice
1 teaspoon salt
1 bunch of cilantro, top only

\*

Throw everything in a blender and blend until onion is chopped completely. This salsa is best made and served within three days, but it will keep for up to two weeks in the refrigerator.

This recipe works well for our Salsa Cream Sauce.

This is our quick and easy version of the time-honored Mexican dip. You can modify the heat by increasing or decreasing the amount of jalapeños or substituting other peppers. This is a great addition to Super Bowl Sunday, when a wide variety of munchies is in order.

# Chili Con Queso

2 tablespoons canola oil
1 cup yellow onion, chopped
1 clove garlic, minced
1–2 jalapeño peppers, seeded and finely chopped
1 small tomato, seeded and chopped
1 4-ounce can green chiles, chopped
½ cup heavy cream
2 cups grated cheddar cheese

\*

In a medium saucepan, heat the oil over medium heat and sauté the onion, garlic, and jalapeños (1 pepper gives a mild flavor, 2 will increase the heat) until they are soft, but not brown, about 8 minutes.

Stir in the tomatoes, green chiles, and cream. Heat through and then reduce the heat to low, stirring in the cheese until melted.

Serve the Chili Con Queso in a fondue pot or small crock-pot to keep it warm. Serve with tortilla chips.

*Makes about 3 cups.*

This cheese spread doubles as a smear on sandwiches or bagels. Even if you're a garlic fanatic, do not add more garlic—it's already at maximum intensity! For those who don't care for goat cheese, you can substitute additional cream cheese.

## Herbed Cheese

1 small clove garlic (trust us, one is enough)
8 ounces goat cheese (or substitute cream cheese)
8 ounces cream cheese, softened
⅛ teaspoon kosher salt
Freshly ground pepper
2 green onions (green tops only), thinly sliced
¼ cup flat leaf parsley, chopped
2 tablespoons fresh basil leaves, chopped
⅓ cup pine nuts, optional

*

Mince the garlic in a food processor. Cut goat and cream cheese into pieces and add to food processor along with salt and pepper to taste. Process until completely combined.

Add onions, parsley, basil, and pine nuts. Pulse until just mixed. Overmixing will turn the mixture green. Alternatively, you can make this in a mixer. Just be sure to mince the garlic well before putting it in the mixture. Serve with crackers.

*Serves 10 to 12.*

# The Least You Need to Know—Gridiron Basics

Not everyone who tunes in to watch the Super Bowl, or regular season games for that matter, is a football expert. The truth is you don't need to know much about the game itself to enjoy it. We've found, however, that even a little knowledge goes a long way toward increasing the excitement, so we've compiled a few facts to help you understand the action a little better.

## The Game and Its Players

Every football game is divided into four quarters with 15 minutes of playing time in each quarter. You're probably wondering why some games seem to go on for hours if there are only 60 minutes to a game. Notice that we said "playing time." The game clock can be stopped for a variety of reasons—a time-out called by either team, an injury on the field, the end of a quarter, and a host of other reasons—including the network's need to put some of that very expensive advertising on the air.

Each team is allowed 11 players on the field at any given time, but there can be as many as 53 active players between the offense, defense, and special team roster during the season. When the offense sets up on the line of scrimmage, it's known as the offensive formation. The defense takes a look at the formation and then sets up its alignment to shut down the offense.

The Offensive Formation

The offense consists of the quarterback, a center, guards, tackles, wide receivers, tight ends, and running backs. The center, guards, and tackles make up the "interior line" of the offense, and it's their job to keep the quarterback safe from very large defensive linemen who wish to sack him. In addition to blocking oncoming defensive linemen, the center "snaps"—or delivers—the ball to the quarterback.

Wide receivers, tight ends, and running backs are eligible to receive the ball from the quarterback, either through a pass reception or by running the ball downfield. Wide receivers tend to be more slightly built and faster runners and dominate the passing game. Tight ends and running backs are bigger and usually run the ball. They're fast but also sturdy enough to take the punishing physical contact that's part of the running game. You'll sometimes hear running backs referred to as halfbacks or fullbacks.

The Defensive Alignment

The defense includes defensive tackles, defensive ends, linebackers, cornerbacks, and safeties. The tackles line up right in the middle of the line of scrimmage, facing the center. They are very large men who can weigh in at almost 300 pounds. The plan is to break through the offensive guards and tackles and get to the guy with the ball—either the quarterback or the running back. Sometimes you'll hear the defensive tackles referred to as nose tackles. The defensive ends line up just to the outside of the tackles. They weigh in at a measly 280 pounds or so. Like the defensive tackles, their job is to flush the quarterback out of "the pocket" and sack him. If the quarterback has already passed the ball to the running back, they tackle the running back and stop forward progress of the ball.

Linebackers are the wild cards on the defense. They position themselves behind the tackles and defensive ends and watch carefully as the ball is snapped. They're looking for any holes in the offensive line so that they can run through and get to the quarterback. Weighing in at a lithe 215 to 270 pounds, they have more speed than the tackles and ends.

The cornerbacks and safeties are responsible for shutting down the passing game. How do they do that? They line up directly across from the wide receivers and the tight ends. They set up behind the linebackers so they have a head start when the quarterback passes to a wide receiver who is sprinting downfield. Once the ball has been received, the plan is to stop the receiver in his tracks.

## Football Talk

Now that you know who's who on the team, the next step is to learn the language. This knowledge not only helps you understand the game but opens up a whole new world of conversation around the dinner table, water cooler, and neighborhood pub.

**Down:** The team playing offense has four chances to move the ball at least 10 yards. Each try is called a down. If they move the ball 10 yards, they get to start counting again, and you'll hear the announcer say, "It's first down and 10," or in the shortened version, "It's first and 10."

**Extra Point:** After a touchdown, the kicker comes onto the field and gets one chance to kick the ball over the goal post for 1 extra point.

**Flag:** A little yellow handkerchief with a weight sewn into it that officials use to call a penalty is a flag. A "flag on the play" means somebody did something bad. We always hope it's the other team.

**Gridiron:** How insiders refer to the football field, so called because of the grid pattern formed by the yard lines.

**Huddle:** The committee meeting that takes place among the offensive players before the play so they can all agree on what they want to do.

**Red Zone:** The last 20 yards before the end zone. It's called that because the defensive team is on red alert for an imminent score.

**Sack:** The quarterback is knocked down before he gets a chance to pass or throw the ball. This usually results in a loss of yards and is very embarrassing for the guys who were supposed to protect the quarterback.

**Line of Scrimmage:** Technically there are two lines of scrimmage for each play, one for each team, separated by the length of the ball. Neither team can cross this line prior to the snap of the ball, which signifies the start of the play.

**Snap:** When the center hikes the ball to the quarterback or a punter, it's called the snap.

**Pocket:** When you hear the announcer say, "He's in the pocket," it means the quarterback is in a safe zone or pocket surrounded by the interior line of the offense—the center, guards, and tackles—and is preparing to throw the ball to a receiver.

## Flag on the Play

Football wouldn't be football if each team didn't try to get away with breaking the rules sometimes. When they get caught, however, it's called a penalty. Some of the most common include the following:

**False Start:** An offensive player, usually a lineman, moves before the ball is snapped.

**Face Mask:** It is considered bad form, and costs a penalty, to grab the face mask of any player while trying to wrestle him to the ground.

**Holding:** When an offensive player uses his hands or arms to impede a defensive player who is attempting to impede an offensive player. Most often this means that an offensive lineman hooks his arm around a defensive lineman who is trying to sack the quarterback.

**Illegal Motion:** Only one player (the *man-in-motion*) is allowed to move prior to the snap, and the motion must be parallel to the line of scrimmage. This penalty is most often called when an offensive player moves forward or comes out of his stance before the ball is snapped.

**Offside:** Each team must be lined up on their line of scrimmage and cannot break the neutral zone. The neutral zone is the area between the front and back of the ball. Most often, this penalty is called when any part of a defensive player's body crosses into the neutral zone prior to the snap.

**Roughing the Passer:** An overly enthusiastic defensive player hits the quarterback after he has passed or thrown the ball.

**Pass Interference:** A defensive player interferes with a receiver's attempt to catch the ball. The receiver can only be stomped on after he's caught the ball.

There are dozens of books that explain the intricacies of the game in much more detail. If you decide you really want to understand the difference between Hang Time and Hand-off, check out your local library or bookstore for more information.

# Gridiron Grilling

## Tailgate and Backyard BBQ Favorites

The minute Neanderthal man harnessed the power of fire and figured out how to cook up a mastodon, the art of grilling was born. Of course, it would be a few years before technology would catch up and offer some handy conveniences. In 1920, Henry Ford—needing a profitable way to dispose of wood scraps and sawdust from his car factory—created the charcoal briquette by chipping wood into small pieces, grinding the wood into powder, and adding a binding agent to create the briquette pillow we use today. A distant relative of Ford's, E. G. Kingsford, later bought the invention and put it into commercial production.

In 1952 George Stephen, a metalworker by trade, inherited a controlling interest in the Weber Brothers Metal Spinning Company, a maker of harbor buoys. Frustrated by the rudimentary brazier-style grills of the day, Stephen refashioned the buoy by cutting it along its equator, adding vents in the sides to control temperature, and using the top as a lid. With the addition of a grate, the modern grill was born—and not a minute too soon.

As veterans returned from World War II in the 1940s, middle-class families moved out in droves into the spacious and affordable suburbs. Backyard grilling became a popular way of entertaining, and by the early 1950s grilling recipes started appearing in mainstream publications like *Good Housekeeping* and *Better Homes & Gardens*.

Now a thriving business with its own cultural icons—including Bobby Flay, Steven Raichlen, and Chris Schlesinger—grilling is easier than ever to master. Modern grills, both charcoal and gas, offer temperature gauges, timers, and multi-tiered grates to eliminate any guesswork, and assorted grilling gadgets make marinating, basting, and flipping easy.

This chapter includes grill recipes we think are the most football-friendly. Many of the dishes marinate overnight and go on the grill during halftime. Of course, tailgate events involve grilled foods almost exclusively, and any of these recipes would be great choices for a pregame party at the stadium.

Remoulade is one of those versatile sauces that go with just about anything. Our favorite way is on steak, hot off the grill. The sauce can be made up to five days in advance, so it's perfect football fare. It will keep for weeks without the parsley, which can be added at the last minute.

# Steak Bites with Remoulade Sauce

1 pound or more of your favorite beef, cut into steaks for
   grilling (beef tenderloin works well)
1 tablespoon canola oil or vegetable oil
Kosher salt and freshly ground pepper to taste

   ✳

Heat the grill to medium-high heat. Rub steaks with oil and sprinkle generously with kosher salt and pepper to your taste.

Sear meat a few minutes on each side until steaks are medium-rare. Remove from heat and cut meat into 1" cubes.

Serve warm with toothpicks and remoulade sauce. If grilling is not your thing, you can trim the steak into bite-sized pieces and sear in a hot pan.

## Remoulade sauce

1 cup mayonnaise
¼ cup Creole mustard or stone-ground mustard
Juice from 1 lemon (about ¼ cup)
¼ teaspoon cayenne pepper
1 anchovy, minced, optional
¼ teaspoon freshly ground black pepper
2 teaspoons capers, drained and chopped
2 tablespoons ketchup
¼ teaspoon of your favorite hot sauce, or more to taste
½ bunch flat leaf parsley, chopped (about ⅓ cup)

   ✳

In a medium bowl, mix all ingredients together.

Store in the refrigerator in a canning jar instead of a plastic container. The sauce keeps longer.

*Serves 4 with sauce left over.*

"Let's face it, you have to have a slightly recessive gene that has a little something to do with the brain to go out on the football field and beat your head against other human beings on a daily basis."

Tim Green

Inspired by classic fajita recipes, this is a dish we like because the spice rub and salsa can be made in advance and the meal comes together during halftime. Store-bought salsa can be substituted to save time. Serve with garlic bread and grilled zucchini.

# Rib Eye Steaks with Salsa

## Steak Rub

2 tablespoons ancho chili powder

½ teaspoon salt

½ teaspoon black pepper

½ teaspoon onion powder

1 teaspoon garlic powder

½ teaspoon ground cinnamon

1½ pounds boneless rib eye steaks

Juice of 1–2 limes

1 tablespoon vegetable oil

## Salsa

½ cup chopped sweet onion

1 cup seeded and chopped tomatoes

1 serrano chile, seeded and finely chopped

2 tablespoons fresh chopped cilantro

2 tablespoons white wine vinegar

1 teaspoon granulated sugar

¼ teaspoon Worcestershire sauce

¼ teaspoon Tabasco sauce

Salt and freshly ground pepper

\*

Preheat the grill (gas or charcoal) to medium-high. In a medium bowl, combine the chili powder, salt, pepper, onion powder, garlic powder, and cinnamon. In another bowl, mix together the salsa ingredients and let sit at room temperature while grilling the steaks.

Brush the meat on both sides with the lime juice, then rub with the spice mixture. Grill the steaks 5 to 6 minutes on each side for medium-rare.

Remove the steaks from the grill and let rest for at least 5 minutes. Serve with the salsa on the side.

*Serves 4.*

Vince Lombardi's Green Bay Packers defeated the Kansas City Chiefs 35–10 in Los Angeles in January 1967 in the first Super Bowl. The game was then known as the AFC-NFC Championship until its third year, when it became known as the Super Bowl.

These beef kabobs work as either an entrée or an appetizer. Marinate the meat overnight in the refrigerator and grill just before serving. We like to offer Corn Soufflé and Gridiron Green Bean Salad with this dish.

# Beef Kabobs with Hoisin Marinade

¼ cup hoisin sauce

3 tablespoons dry sherry

2 tablespoons soy sauce

2 teaspoons sesame oil

2 tablespoons minced green onions

2 cloves garlic, minced

1 teaspoon fresh minced ginger

1 teaspoon granulated sugar

1 teaspoon salt

1½ pounds flank steak, cut across the grain on a diagonal into ½" slices.

✳

In a medium bowl combine the first 9 ingredients. Place the meat in a large resealable plastic bag and pour the marinade mixture over the slices, turning to coat. Refrigerate at least 3 hours, or overnight, turning occasionally.

If using wooden skewers, soak them in water for at least 30 minutes. Oil the grill grate and preheat grill to high heat.

Thread flank steak strips on skewers. Grill 3 minutes per side or to desired doneness.

*Serves 4 to 6.*

These big, juicy, well-flavored burgers are early season favorites for us. Combine the ingredients and refrigerate before kick-off, then grill them up during halftime. We serve the burgers with potato salad and big dill pickles.

# Halftime Beer Burgers

2 pounds ground beef
¼ cup Sam Adams or other lager beer, at room temperature
3 teaspoons stone-ground mustard
2 teaspoons dried oregano
Salt and pepper to taste
4 kaiser rolls or hamburger buns, split

   \*

In a large bowl, combine the beef, beer, mustard, and seasonings. Cover and refrigerate for at least 10 minutes.

Divide the mixture into 4 patties, each about 1" thick. Cook the patties on the grill, 4 minutes per side for medium-rare.

If you want cheeseburgers, add a slice of sharp cheddar cheese to the top of the patties about 1 minute before they are done. Let the cheese melt over the top and sides of the patty.

Serve on split kaiser rolls or hamburger buns.

*Serves 4.*

> The only team ever to go undefeated is the 1972 Miami Dolphins, with a record of 17-0-0, capping that season off triumphantly with a victory in Super Bowl VII, behind such stars as Bob Griese, Paul Warfield, Larry Csonka, Jim Kiick and Nick Buoniconti.

This recipe gets its name from the Spanish word *pincho*, referring to small cubes of meat, seasoned and grilled on skewers. This version uses lamb, which is popular in Morocco, but pork works as well. The meat marinates overnight—then you just put the cubes on skewers and grill them at halftime. Serve with potato salad and Sangria.

# Lamb Pinchitos

¼ cup olive oil
2 cloves garlic, minced
1 tablespoon cilantro, minced
½ teaspoon ground cumin, optional
1 teaspoon paprika
½ teaspoon dried thyme
½ teaspoon turmeric
2 tablespoons red wine vinegar
½ teaspoon salt
½ teaspoon freshly ground pepper
1–1½ pounds lamb, cut into 1" cubes
1 lemon, quartered, optional

＊

In a large bowl, whisk together the oil, garlic, cilantro, cumin, paprika, thyme, turmeric, vinegar, salt, and pepper. Add the lamb cubes and toss to coat.

Pour the mixture into a large resealable plastic bag and marinate for at least 4 hours or overnight in the refrigerator, turning occasionally.

Preheat the grill to medium-high. If using wooden skewers, soak them in water for 30 minutes.

Thread the lamb chunks onto the skewers and grill for 10 to 12 minutes, turning once, until the meat is medium-rare.

Serve the Pinchitos on the skewers with the lemon quarters on the side. Guests have the option of squeezing the lemon over the meat.

*Serves 4 to 6.*

Souvlaki may actually be one of the original tailgate foods. Served by street vendors in Constantinople during public events, the dish combines grilled meat, pita, and dill sauce. Our version was developed to work around halftime, but we don't think the ancient Greeks would mind.

---

# Grilled Souvlaki in Pita

¼ cup red wine
¼ cup olive oil
1½ teaspoons lemon juice
1 teaspoon dried oregano
1 clove garlic, minced
½ teaspoon freshly ground pepper
2 teaspoons salt
2 pounds lamb, cut into 1" chunks
8 pita bread rounds
3 tablespoons olive oil

## Yogurt Dill Sauce

1 cucumber, peeled, seeded and grated
1 teaspoon salt
2 cups plain yogurt
¼ teaspoon dried dill
1 clove garlic, minced
Pepper to taste

\*

In a large bowl, combine the red wine, olive oil, lemon juice, oregano, garlic, pepper, and salt. Add the lamb chunks and toss to coat. Cover and refrigerate for at least 2 hours or up to 2 days, turning occasionally.

In a small bowl, combine the cucumber and salt and allow to sit for 15 minutes. Squeeze the excess moisture out of the cucumber.

In a clean bowl, combine the cucumber, yogurt, dill, garlic, and pepper. Keep refrigerated until the lamb is ready to serve.

Soak wooden skewers in water for 30 minutes or use metal skewers. Lightly oil the grate and preheat the grill to medium-high. Thread the lamb chunks onto the skewers and grill for 10 minutes, turning once. Take the meat off the grill and allow to rest for 5 minutes.

Brush the pita bread with olive oil and carefully warm on the grill, about 1 minute. Serve the lamb with the pita bread and yogurt sauce.

*Serves 6 to 8.*

"Football is not a contact sport. Dancing is a contact sport. Football is a collision sport."

Robert Zuppke

This is great football fare because the Pico de Gallo and Baja Sauce can be made in advance of the game. At halftime, grill up the fish and serve with tortillas. Coleslaw is a nice side dish.

---

# Fish Tacos
## Pico de Gallo

1 red bell pepper, finely chopped
3 tomatoes, finely chopped
½ red onion, finely chopped
1–2 jalapeños, finely chopped
2–3 tablespoons cilantro, minced
¾ teaspoon salt
2 tablespoons fresh lime juice

## Baja Sauce

1 cup sour cream
¼ cup buttermilk
½ teaspoon ground cumin, optional
½ teaspoon chili powder
Pinch cayenne, optional
      *

3 pounds grouper or other firm white fish
Salt and pepper to taste
Flour tortillas (12–15 tortillas for 6 people, depending on the
    size of tortillas you use)
      *

Lightly oil the grate and heat the grill to medium-high.

In a medium bowl, combine red bell pepper, tomatoes, onion, jalapeños, cilantro, salt, and lime juice. Set aside.

In another medium bowl, combine the sour cream, buttermilk, cumin, chili powder, and the optional cayenne.

Season the fish with salt and pepper. Grill until the flesh is opaque inside and flakes easily, about 4 minutes per side. Cooking time will depend on the thickness and density of the fish.

Serve the fish along with the Pico de Gallo, Baja Sauce, and tortillas.

*Serves 6.*

A deaf football player who used sign language to communicate plays inspired the "huddle" in 1894. His team didn't want the opposition to see the signals he used, so they turned to huddle around him.

Recreated from a memorable meal at a San Francisco restaurant, this dish wins rave reviews at every party. Rich and hearty, salmon grills up quickly so we don't miss any game time. Serve with flavored rice and steamed sugar snap peas.

---

# Grilled Scotch Salmon

Grated zest of 1 orange
¾ cup orange juice
½ cup Scotch
2 tablespoons honey
1½ tablespoons Dijon mustard
3 teaspoons Worcestershire sauce
1½ teaspoons freshly ground pepper
1 teaspoon salt
6 salmon fillets or steaks, 6–8 ounces each

\*

In a medium bowl, combine the orange zest, orange juice, Scotch, honey, mustard, Worcestershire sauce, pepper, and salt and whisk together.

Place the salmon in a shallow baking dish and pour the marinade over the fish. Cover and refrigerate at least 3 hours and up to 6 hours, turning the salmon at least once.

Lightly oil the grill and preheat to medium-high.

Remove the salmon from the marinade and grill about 5 minutes each side, turning once. The salmon is done when the flesh is opaque and flakes easily.

*Serves 6.*

> "There are two kinds of people in the world:
> Notre Dame lovers and Notre Dame haters. And,
> quite frankly, they're both a pain in the ass."
>
> Dan Devine, former Notre Dame coach

This recipe resulted from a store-bought marinade mix gone wrong. Kellie's friend Diana loved the sound of a cinnamon rosemary marinade, but the stuff proved too salty, with only a hint of cinnamon and rosemary flavors. Undeterred, Diana created her own version and kindly shared it with us. Serve with pickled beets and grilled potatoes.

# Cinnamon Rosemary Chicken

1 cup olive oil
2 tablespoons dried rosemary
2½ tablespoons ground cinnamon
1 bay leaf
1 tablespoon whole peppercorns
1 teaspoon coarse sea salt
½ teaspoon cracked black pepper
2 tablespoons fresh lime juice
2 tablespoons balsamic vinegar
2½ pounds chicken breasts, thighs, and/or drumsticks

*

In a large resealable plastic bag, combine the olive oil, rosemary, cinnamon, bay leaf, peppercorns, salt, cracked black pepper, lime juice, and vinegar.

Add the chicken, seal the bag, and carefully turn until the marinade evenly coats the chicken. Refrigerate the chicken for at least 2 hours or overnight.

Preheat the grill to medium-high. Remove the chicken from the marinade and grill for 25 minutes, turning once. Wrap the chicken in a large piece of heavy-duty aluminum foil and let sit for an additional 20 minutes or until chicken reaches an internal temperature of 165°.

*Serves 6.*

While this chicken takes a while to cook, you can put it on the grill before the pregame show and check it during commercial breaks. Serve at halftime with Gridiron Green Bean Salad and Cheesy Potato Casserole.

---

## Beer Can Chicken

1 12-ounce can beer
1 whole roasting chicken
¼ cup canola oil
Kosher salt
Cracked pepper
Grilling wood chips, optional (use the flavor of your choice)

\*

Preheat the grill to medium-high. If using wood chips, pour ⅓ of a can of beer over them in a small bowl to soak.

Remove the neck and giblets from inside the chicken. Rinse the body cavity and dry with paper towels. Season the chicken with canola oil, salt, and pepper.

Put two disposable aluminum pans together and place the beer can with the remaining ⅔ of the beer in the center of the double-thick pan.

Carefully place the seasoned chicken upright with the body cavity on top of the open beer can, pulling out the chicken legs to make a kind of tripod. As the chicken cooks, the beer will steam and infuse a wonderful flavor into the chicken.

Put the wood chips in a wood chip pan for the gas grill or on top of the charcoal briquettes. If using a gas grill, turn the middle burner to low and the two outside burners to medium. If you have only two burners, turn one to low and one to medium. If using charcoal, use barbecue tongs to move the briquettes to one side of the drum, leaving one side free of briquettes.

Place the aluminum pan over the low heat burner or the side of the charcoal drum with no briquettes. Cover the grill and cook for 1 hour and 20 minutes to 1 hour and 30 minutes or until the internal temperature reaches at least 160°. Check on the chicken every 30 minutes.

*Serves 6 to 8.*

Bratwurst is easy to grill, packed with flavor, and the perfect accompaniment to beer. Serve with caramelized onions and stone-ground mustard.

---

## Beer Brats

2 packages of Johnsonville Brats (5 per package)
1 bottle of beer

*

Place brats in a bowl or pan and cover with beer. Let sit for an hour.

Heat grill to medium-high. Grill brats on each side until cooked through, about 15 minutes. Baste with beer occasionally.

If you don't have access to a grill, Beer Brats can also be made in a heavy saucepan. Heat pan and brown brats on each side. Pour beer over brats, cover with a lid, and cook for 15 to 20 minutes over medium-high heat.

*Makes 10 brats, serving 5 to 10.*

We all need a quick and easy no-cook sauce. The best thing about barbecue sauce is that every griller has his or her own signature recipe. Add or change something to make this your own.

# Quick Kick Barbecue Sauce

1 cup ketchup
1 cup chili sauce
1 cup dark brown sugar
¾ cup balsamic or rice wine vinegar
2 tablespoons Coleman's dry mustard
2 tablespoons Pickapeppa or Worcestershire sauce
¼ teaspoon freshly ground pepper

\*

Place all ingredients in a medium bowl and stir until brown sugar is dissolved. Use as a basting sauce for ribs, chicken or pulled pork.

*Makes about 4 cups of sauce.*

# Tips on Tailgating

Once considered a quick bite and a beer in the parking lot before the game, tailgating has blossomed into a cultural phenomenon with all the requisite associations, gadgets, gizmos and gurus to prove it.

True to their ancient rivalry, both Princeton and Yale claim to have initiated modern-day tailgating in the 1800s. Actually, the ritual is a little older than that. Outdoor pregame festivals date back to 300 B.C., when crowds gathered, pitched tents, and roasted oxen prior to the Olympic games. Warm-up activities involved drinking, dancing, flute playing, and sacrifices—your typical tailgate stuff.

Across the southern United States, colleges have raised tailgating to an art form. Ten years ago it was customary to lower the tailgate of a pickup, lay out some foods, crack open a beer, and *voilà*—tailgate party. Today these events start days in advance, when rigs ranging from reconditioned school buses to tricked-out RVs arrive on site, elaborate tents are pitched while professional-grade smokers are fired up, and draft beer is on tap!

The American Tailgater Association estimates that 23 million Americans take part in the pregame festivities each year. The largest tailgate is reported to be the warm-up to the Florida-Georgia match in Jacksonville, known as "the world's largest cocktail party." Fans start arriving on Wednesday for the Saturday game. The game ends on Saturday afternoon—the party ends on Sunday night.

Here are our top tips for organizing a successful tailgate event.

- To transport hot foods, put them in a Dutch oven and line your cooler with a thick layer of newspaper. Tape the pot lid closed to avoid spills. An insulated cooler works just as well for hot foods as it does for cold.

- Store soups, stews, and chilis in thermoses to keep the food warm.

- Have the right equipment. A number of online retailers carry the trappings for tailgating and transporting food for outdoor events, so fire up your search engine and see what you can find. We've invested in thermal gel packs that we keep in the freezer until it's time to leave for the stadium. They can be reused, and they don't make a mess. There are also some great portable barbecues available today, so check those out too.

- Pack the cooler(s) in reverse order so that the items you need first are on top. Also, a full cooler maintains its temperature longer than one that's partially full, so tuck additional ice packs or nonperishable foods in the corners.

- If you use ice, try freezing water in plastic containers or freezer bags and placing them in the cooler. When they melt, the water won't be all over your cooler and you'll have extra water to douse the charcoal after the tailgate.

- Wash and dry salad greens the night before. Wrap them in paper towels and transport them in resealable plastic bags.

- If you're grilling or smoking, set up your grill away from cars and seating areas. Make sure the surface is level. Have water or a fire extinguisher handy in case of emergencies. To dispose of your charcoal safely, generously water a spot on the ground, then dump the coals on this spot and douse with water until you're sure the coals no longer retain heat. Finally, place them in a small garbage pail with a lid and dispose of them later when there is no danger of fire.

- Disposable rubber gloves are very handy—no pun intended. If you're handling raw meat, you simply discard the gloves afterward and don't worry about scrubbing your hands with soap.
- Invest in a good instant-read thermometer. It's invaluable in determining when meats are safe to serve. Chicken should reach an internal temperature of 165° (170° for thighs), pork should be at 160°, lamb at 130° for medium-rare and 140° for medium. Beef should register 145° for medium-rare and 160° for medium.
- Recipes that allow for generous portions are good tailgate options. You never know how many fans you're going to pick up along the way.
- Plastic plates are much sturdier than paper ones, which can get soggy. We always have a generous supply of paper towels, moistened wipes, and garbage bags for easy clean-up.
- Bring extra dressing, salt, and pepper to re-season your dishes just before serving.
- A list can be your best friend for tailgate events. Start with the basics and add to it every tailgate until you have a foolproof checklist for your events.
- Biggest rookie mistake? No chairs. Invest in pop-up camping chairs and you'll be a much happier tailgater.

# Sandwiches

## Hearty Handfuls

Food scholars passionately debate the birth of the modern sandwich. Some claim it was introduced in the first century B.C. by Rabbi Hillel The Elder, who observed Passover by sandwiching chopped nuts, apples, spices, and wine between two matzohs. Others claim that during the Middle Ages, thick slices of bread called trenchers were used in place of plates, with meats and other foods piled on top, to be eaten with fingers. The trenchers—thick, stale, and filled with the grease and juice from the meats—were then discarded to dogs or the poor.

Regardless of their origin, one thing is clear—sandwiches make great football food. Low maintenance, prepared in advance of the pregame show, and easy to eat while leaping around the living room screaming at referees, they are always welcome at our football events. So when you don't want to miss a minute of game time, think sandwiches. Teamed up with soup, they're a game-friendly option that waits for you—not the other way around.

In this chapter, we've included sandwiches that travel well to tailgate events as well as hot sandwiches that hit the spot late in the season for an easy cold weather *Monday Night Football* dinner. To transport hot sandwiches to the stadium or a friend's house, wrap them in aluminum foil while they're still warm and transport them in a newspaper-lined cooler, which keeps things hot as well as cold.

Inspired by the famous New Orleans muffaletta, this is the ultimate tailgate sandwich. Kellie makes it on Friday night and transports it in a cooler to Saturday afternoon stadium games. Serve with coleslaw and red wine.

---

# Muffaletta Tailgater

## Relish

1½ cups chopped pimento-stuffed olives

1 cup chopped olives

3 anchovies, chopped

2 tablespoons capers, drained

⅔ cup olive oil

2 tablespoons lemon juice

⅓ cup minced parsley

2 cloves garlic, minced

1 teaspoon dried oregano

*

1 8-inch circular loaf of French bread

⅔ pound sliced salami

⅔ pound provolone cheese

⅔ pound sliced mortadella

⅓ pound prosciutto

*

In a small bowl, combine the relish ingredients. Cover and chill for 2 hours or up to 2 days.

Split the bread in half horizontally. Remove enough of the soft inside to make room for the meats, leaving a ¾-inch shell.

Brush some of the relish inside the top of the bread shell, then spoon half of the mixture on the bottom round of bread. Arrange the salami, provolone, mortadella, and prosciutto in layers inside the bottom bread shell.

Spread the remaining relish on top of the last layer and cover with the top shell. Wrap the sandwich tightly in plastic wrap, then place in a pan with something to weight it down—a heavy skillet works well. Refrigerate for at least 1 hour. Slice the sandwich into wedges and serve.

*Serves 6 to 8.*

Upon receiving a 15-yard penalty from referee Jim Durfee, George Halas yelled, "You stink!"

After marching off an additional 15-yard penalty, Jim Durfee replied, "How do I smell from here?"

Classic comfort food, served on a bun with creamy Blue Cheese Dressing, this dish is guaranteed to liven up your spirits if too many of your players end up on the injured list. Make the meatloaf over the weekend and gently reheat for the perfect *Monday Night Football* dinner.

---

# Meatloaf Sandwich with Blue Cheese Dressing

1 pound ground beef
½ pound ground pork
½ pound ground veal (substitute ½ pound ground beef if
    ground veal is unavailable)
1 cup bread crumbs
1 small onion, chopped finely
1 egg
1 cup milk
½ cup chopped flat leaf parsley
1 teaspoon dried thyme
2 tablespoons chili sauce
1 tablespoon prepared horseradish
1 teaspoon dry mustard
1 teaspoon salt
½ teaspoon freshly ground black pepper
6 kaiser rolls

## Blue Cheese Dressing

⅔ cup mayonnaise
⅓ cup sour cream
1 cup blue cheese, crumbled
Salt and pepper to taste

\*

Preheat the oven to 375°.

In a large bowl, thoroughly combine the meats, bread crumbs, onion, egg, milk, parsley, thyme, chili sauce, horseradish, mustard, salt and pepper.

Pat the mixture into a 9 × 5-inch loaf pan. Bake for 1 hour, or until the meatloaf is richly browned on top and a meat thermometer inserted into the center of the loaf registers 155°. Let the meatloaf stand for 10 minutes. (When cool, you can cover and refrigerate the meatloaf; gently reheat the next day at 325° for about 20 minutes.)

In a nonreactive bowl, combine the mayonnaise, sour cream, and blue cheese. Season to taste with salt and pepper. The dressing can be made up to three days ahead and refrigerated in an airtight container.

Cut the kaiser rolls in half horizontally and toast. Cut the warm meatloaf into 1" thick slices and place on the kaiser rolls. Top with 1 to 2 tablespoons of the blue cheese dressing.

*Serves 6.*

> "Trying to maintain order during a legalized gang brawl involving 80 toughs with a little whistle, a hanky and a ton of prayer."
>
> Anonymous NFL referee explaining his job

Maili wasn't a Philly Cheese Steak fan until she moved to Pennsylvania and tried the real thing at a stadium game. But she couldn't figure out why they took so long to make—until she realized the secret. The difference between a beef and onion sandwich and a great Philly Cheese Steak is waiting for the onions to release their sugar and then caramelize. The moral of the story? Make these at halftime.

# Philly Cheese Steak Sandwiches

3 tablespoons canola oil
1 medium yellow onion (about 10 ounces), thinly sliced
Pinch of kosher salt
½ green bell pepper, thinly sliced
2 cups mushrooms, thinly sliced
10 ounces beef of your choice, very thinly sliced
½ teaspoon salt
⅛ teaspoon freshly ground pepper, or more to taste
4 slices provolone cheese, or white American cheese
2 sandwich rolls

*

Heat 1 tablespoon canola oil in a large frying pan on medium-high heat. Add the onion, sprinkle with kosher salt, and cook for 3 minutes, stirring occasionally. Add sliced bell pepper and stir until slightly softened, about 3 minutes. Add mushrooms and another tablespoon of canola oil, and sprinkle with another pinch of salt. Cook for about 5 to 7 minutes on medium heat until vegetables are nicely browned. Remove the cooked vegetables to a side dish.

Season the beef with salt and pepper. Put the remaining tablespoon of canola oil in the hot pan and cook the beef quickly, until browned. Add the reserved onion mixture to the beef. Divide into two piles in the pan (one for each sandwich) and turn off the heat. Place 2 slices of cheese on top of each pile of hot meat and allow to melt. Scoop the melted cheese and meat into sandwich rolls and serve immediately.

*Makes 2 sandwiches.*

The two things we like best about Thanksgiving are football games all day and leftovers. Here's one of our favorite ways to use up the turkey and cranberry sauce—trust us on the pesto!

# After Thanksgiving Day Sandwich

4 French bread sandwich rolls
¼ cup pesto
1 pound roast turkey, sliced
½ pound provolone cheese, sliced
¾–1 cup cranberry sauce

*

Preheat the oven to 350°.

Slice the sandwich rolls and spread one side of each roll with the pesto. Layer the turkey and cheese slices on the sandwich. Cover the remaining side of the sandwich rolls with cranberry sauce and place on top of the other half.

Wrap each sandwich in aluminum foil. Place foil packets on a cookie sheet and bake for 12 to 14 minutes or until cheese is melted and sandwich is heated through.

*Makes 4 sandwiches*

"Thanksgiving dinners take eighteen hours to prepare. They are consumed in twelve minutes. Halftime takes twelve minutes. This is not a coincidence."

Erma Bombeck

Legend has it that the Reuben was created in 1914 for one of Charlie Chaplin's leading ladies. Announcing she was so hungry she could "eat a brick," she asked a New York deli master named Reuben to make her a special sandwich, and this classic was born. Our Indianapolis version uses sauerkraut, but New Yorkers substitute coleslaw.

## The Classic Reuben

8 slices dark rye bread
⅔ pound thinly sliced corned beef
½ cup sauerkraut, drained
⅓ pound thinly sliced Swiss cheese
⅓ cup Thousand Island dressing
2 tablespoons butter

\*

Layer the corned beef on 4 of the bread slices and top with the sauerkraut and Swiss cheese. Spread the dressing over the cheese and top with the remaining bread slices.

Heat the butter in a heavy skillet over medium heat. When the butter begins to bubble, place the sandwiches in the pan and cook until the bread is well browned, about 4 minutes. Turn the sandwiches over and brown the other side. Cut in half and serve hot.

*Makes 4 sandwiches.*

The first televised game took place on December 28, 1958. Forty-five million viewers tuned in to see the Baltimore Colts defeat the New York Giants, 23–17, in a sudden death overtime in the NFL championship game.

The Cubano is the Cuban version of a ham and cheese sandwich, brought to the United States by Cuban-Americans. The sandwich is traditionally served on Cuban bread, but we prefer Ciabatta, which has a crunchier texture.

## Cubano Sandwich

⅓ cup red wine vinegar
⅓ cup orange juice
¼ cup olive oil
1 clove garlic, minced
½ teaspoon salt
½ teaspoon freshly ground pepper
1 pork tenderloin, about 1 pound, trimmed of excess fat
1 loaf Cuban, French or Ciabatta bread
½ pound baked ham, thinly sliced
½ pound Baby Swiss cheese
Yellow or deli mustard
8 dill pickle slices

\*

Combine the vinegar, orange juice, olive oil, garlic, salt, and pepper and pour into a large resealable plastic bag.

Place the pork tenderloin in the bag and allow to marinate in the refrigerator for at least 2 hours, occasionally flipping the bag over to distribute the marinade evenly.

Preheat the oven to 350°. Remove the pork from the marinade and place in small roasting pan.

Roast for 20 to 30 minutes or until internal temperature reaches 160°. Allow to rest for 15 minutes, then slice the pork thinly.

Slice the bread in half horizontally and spread a thin layer of mustard on the top and bottom halves. Layer the pork tenderloin slices, Baby Swiss, baked ham, and pickle slices and cover the sandwiches with the top half of the bread. Slice each sandwich in half and then slice each half lengthwise.

Heat a griddle or large frying pan to medium. Place the sandwiches on the hot griddle and cover with a heavy skillet to flatten them. Grill the sandwiches 3 to 4 minutes per side or until the cheese is melted and the bread is golden brown. Serve immediately.

*Makes 4 sandwiches.*

This is great comfort food if your team's chances at a Wild Card spot are hopeless. They're not called "sloppy" for nothing, so make sure to have plenty of napkins on hand.

---

## Our Favorite Sloppy Joes

2 pounds ground beef
1 onion, chopped
2 ribs celery, chopped
1 12-ounce bottle tomato-based chili sauce
1 8-ounce can tomato sauce
2 teaspoons Worcestershire sauce
1½ teaspoons salt
½ teaspoon freshly ground pepper
1 tablespoon dark brown sugar
½ teaspoon chili powder
8 hamburger or kaiser rolls, toasted

＊

In a heavy skillet over medium heat, cook the meat, onions, and celery until the meat is browned and the onion is tender. Drain off the excess fat. Add the chili and tomato sauces, Worcestershire, salt, pepper, brown sugar, and chili powder.

Lower the heat and simmer, uncovered, until the liquid is reduced and the mixture is thick, about 25 to 30 minutes. Serve over toasted hamburger buns.

*Serves 8.*

Tomatillos resemble small green tomatoes. You may find fresh tomatillos in the produce section, in thin papery husks. We've included this recipe because so many mainstream markets now carry canned varieties, which save time. If you can't find tomatillos, use whole tomatoes.

## Chili Verde Burritos

4 pounds pork tenderloin, cubed
2 tablespoons olive oil
1 onion, chopped
3 cloves garlic, minced
1 teaspoon dried oregano, preferably Mexican
1 teaspoon ground cumin, optional
2 12-ounce cans tomatillos, drained, halved
4 4-ounce cans green chiles, chopped
1 teaspoon salt
Flour tortillas

*

Cover the meat with cold water, bring to a boil, reduce heat, cover, and simmer about 40 minutes or until the meat is very tender. Drain the meat.

Heat oil in a heavy skillet over medium heat. Add pork, onion, and garlic and cook until vegetables are soft, about 5 minutes. Add the oregano, cumin, tomatillos, chiles, and salt.

Cover and cook 10 minutes over medium-high heat. Reduce heat, uncover, and simmer gently for 20 minutes. Serve with warm flour tortillas.

As suggested sides and for additional fillings, we recommend rice, beans, salsa, grated cheese, guacamole, chopped onions, cilantro, and sour cream.

*Serves 8.*

# Any Given Sunday

## Morning Specials for Early Games

In 1948 there were 172,000 television sets in the United States. By 1954 that number had skyrocketed to 25 million. CBS dominated the industry with entertainment programming, but sports coverage remained an afterthought, viewed by the networks as a necessary evil. However, the NFL—with the marketing savvy that would eventually propel the sport into the prime time stratosphere—saw the future and resolved to put professional football on the air.

Game shows and news programs held the morning slots, with soap operas dominating the afternoon and entertainment shows covering prime time. But Sunday afternoon, nicknamed "the ghetto" by station executives, was resistant to programming. Under the artful direction of Commissioner Bert Bell, NFL franchise owners inked a deal with CBS to broadcast every away game, in each market, while blacking out home games to protect gate ticket sales. Enter the NFL Sunday game and Bell's famous adage, "On any given Sunday, any team in our league can beat any other team," providing eager fans with a new way to enjoy the day of rest.

For the early Sunday pro game, we love to invite friends over and enjoy some morning food. We've included our favorites in this chapter—recipes that are easy to prepare and won't interfere with game watching time. Our Cheese Strata and Caramel French Toast can be assembled the night before and tucked in the oven before kick-off. Most mainstream markets now carry precut fresh fruit, which makes a great side dish with no additional work for the cook. So stir up some Bloody Hail Marys, put out a dish of cocktail nuts, and enjoy America's game.

Just by looking at the ingredient list you can tell these eggs are easy to make. Baked eggs give us flexibility that scrambled eggs just don't allow. Assemble the eggs in the muffin tin before the game and keep covered in the refrigerator. When guests arrive, preheat the oven, pop them in, and watch the game until the timer goes off. Serve with coffee cake and some sliced fruit.

# Baked Eggs

6 slices Black Forest ham
6 eggs
6 teaspoons half-and-half
Seasoning salt to taste
4 tablespoons grated cheddar cheese

*

Preheat the oven to 450°. Spray 6 muffin tins with nonstick cooking spray or lightly oil.

Fit one slice of ham into each muffin cup (ends will stick up and hang over edges of cups.) Crack one raw egg on top of each piece of ham. Cover each egg with 1 teaspoon half-and-half, season with seasoning salt, and cover with 2 teaspoons of cheddar cheese.

Bake for 10 minutes. Carefully remove eggs from tin and serve.

*Serves 6.*

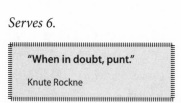

"When in doubt, punt."
Knute Rockne

Cheese Stratas are to football brunch parties what linebackers are to the defense. These recipes are the backbone of your game plan to serve great food and not miss the game. Made the night before and tucked in the oven before kick-off, they are no fuss, no muss, and everyone loves them. You can also bake them at home for transport to a friend's house in a newspaper-lined cooler. Serve with fruit and Glazed Bacon.

# Cheese Strata

12 slices bread, cubed

2¼ cups grated cheese

1 cup cooked, diced ham, optional

½ pound fresh mushrooms, thinly sliced, optional

2 cups half-and-half

12 eggs

6 tablespoons butter, melted

2 teaspoons Dijon mustard

½ teaspoon salt

½ teaspoon freshly ground pepper

*

Preheat the oven to 350°. Butter an 11 × 13-inch casserole dish.

Arrange the bread cubes across the bottom. Sprinkle the cheese on top. The optional ham and mushrooms can be layered with the cheese, for variety.

In a blender or food processor, combine the half-and-half, eggs, butter, mustard, and salt and pepper. Pour over the bread and cheese mixture; cover and refrigerate overnight.

Bake 45 to 55 minutes or until firm in the center and puffed.

*Serves 6 to 8.*

This recipe has been a Christmas morning tradition at Kellie's house for years, but it's also an excellent choice if you have friends coming over for the early Sunday game. Prepare the cheese and chile layers the night before and pour the custard over the top at the last minute. You can use store-bought salsa to save time, but our Mango Salsa is really something special.

---

# Chile Rellenos Strata

2–2½ pounds Monterey Jack cheese, cut into ½" strips
2 4-ounce cans chopped green chiles (or 1 cup freshly roasted and chopped chiles)
3 eggs
2 cups whole milk
½ cup flour
½ teaspoon salt

## Mango Salsa

2 cups fresh tomatoes, chopped
1 cup canned crushed tomatoes
¼ cup chopped yellow onion
2 green onions, thinly sliced
1–2 fresh jalapeños, seeded and minced
2 teaspoons fresh lime juice
¼ cup fresh cilantro, chopped
1 fresh mango chopped or 1 cup jarred mango, drained and chopped
¼ teaspoon ground cumin, optional
¼ teaspoon dried Mexican oregano
¼ teaspoon salt

\*

Preheat the oven to 350°.

Layer the cheese and green chiles in a 9 × 13-inch baking dish. (You can substitute jalapeños if you like your strata spicy.)

In a medium bowl or blender, beat together the eggs, milk, flour, and salt. Pour the mixture over the cheese.

Bake for 45 to 55 minutes or until the top is golden brown and puffed. Let stand for 10 minutes before cutting into squares. Serve with the salsa on the side.

For the salsa, in a medium bowl combine the tomatoes, onions, jalapeños, lime juice, cilantro, fruit, cumin, oregano, and salt. Cover and chill.

*Serves 6 to 8.*

In December 1978, after fifteen years without a championship, New York Giants fans decided to take matters into their own hands. First they hanged the team owner in effigy during a game and lit a bonfire with their season tickets. When that didn't work, they tried to rename the team the New York Gnomes and attempted to sue the management for nonsupport. Alas, the Giants finished that year with a 6–10 record.

With deep, rich flavors that celebrate the fall season, this French Toast is incredibly game-friendly because you make it the night before and bake it before serving. No last minute dipping and frying of bread slices! Serve with Glazed Bacon and a Waldorf salad.

## Caramel French Toast

1 stick unsalted butter
1 cup brown sugar, lightly packed
2 tablespoons corn syrup
1 French baguette, cut into 1½" slices
5 large eggs
1½ cups half-and-half
1 teaspoon vanilla
2 tablespoons brandy, optional
¼ teaspoon salt

✳

In a small, heavy saucepan, melt the butter with the sugar and corn syrup until sugar is dissolved. Pour into a 9 × 13-inch baking dish and coat the bottom of the dish evenly.

Arrange bread in a single layer in the baking dish, flipping once or twice to coat the bread completely with the sugar mixture.

In a bowl, whisk the eggs, half-and-half, vanilla, optional brandy, and salt. Pour mixture evenly over bread slices and let sit for at least an hour or up to a day, covered and refrigerated.

Bake, uncovered, at 350° for 35 minutes. Serve immediately.

*Serves 8 to 10.*

Although this dish can't be made too far in advance, it goes together quickly, so it can be served right before kick-off or during halftime for the early game. Serve with scrambled eggs and sausages.

# Apple Cinnamon Dutch Baby

6 tablespoons butter
¼ cup granulated sugar
2 teaspoons ground cinnamon
¼ teaspoon nutmeg
2 Granny Smith apples, peeled and thinly sliced
4 large eggs
1 cup flour
1 cup milk
Powdered sugar

\*

Preheat the oven to 425º.

In a heavy, ovenproof 12-inch skillet (cast iron works well), melt the butter over medium-high heat. Add the sugar, cinnamon, and nutmeg and stir to combine. Add the apple slices and cook, stirring occasionally, until the apples are soft, about 5 minutes. Place the skillet in the oven and bake for 5 minutes.

In a blender or food processor, beat the eggs and the flour, then add the milk and blend until well combined. Pour the batter over the baked apples, return to the oven, and bake until puffed and golden brown, about 15 minutes.

Dust the Dutch Baby with powdered sugar and serve.

*Serves 6.*

> "I wouldn't ever set out to hurt anyone deliberately unless it was, you know, important—like a league game or something."
>
> Dick Butkus, former Chicago Bears Lineman

We love this recipe because it's so versatile. Use it as a delicious finger food before the first quarter, or serve with scrambled eggs and a fruit platter for the perfect Sunday early game brunch.

---

# Hot Crab Quesadillas

1½ cups grated Monterey Jack cheese
2 ounces cream cheese, room temperature
¼ cup fresh cilantro, chopped
2 tablespoons orange juice
Salt and pepper to taste
6–8 ounces crabmeat, drained
¾ cup seeded and chopped plum tomatoes
½ cup chopped green onions
1 tablespoon seeded and minced jalapeño pepper
Salt and pepper to taste
4 7"–8" flour tortillas
4 tablespoons vegetable oil

∗

In a medium bowl, mix the cheeses, cilantro, and orange juice. Season with salt and pepper. (This can be made a day ahead, covered and chilled. Bring to room temperature before continuing.)

In a medium bowl, mix together the crab, tomatoes, green onion, and jalapeño. Spread the cheese mixture over half of each tortilla. Spoon the crabmeat mixture on top of the cheese mixture, dividing equally. Sprinkle with salt and pepper. Fold the tortillas in half and press gently to seal.

In each of 2 heavy large skillets, heat 1 tablespoon oil over medium heat. Working in batches, cook the quesadillas in the skillets until the cheese melts and the tortillas are golden brown, about 3 minutes per side. Add more oil as needed.

Cut the quesadillas into wedges and serve.

*Serves 4 as an entrée.*

This coffee cake recipe can be adapted to your personal taste by adding the fresh fruit of your choice—nectarines, peaches, apples, pears, blueberries or blackberries. Bake it in a rectangular pan with a streusel topping and serve with scrambled eggs for the early game.

# Cinnamon Crunch Coffee Cake

1½ sticks (12 tablespoons) unsalted butter

1½ cups granulated sugar

Zest of 2 lemons

4 eggs, at room temperature

3 cups unbleached white flour

1½ teaspoons baking powder

1½ teaspoons baking soda

½ teaspoon salt

1½ cups sour cream

1 tablespoon pure vanilla extract

2 cups fresh fruit of your choice, optional

## Streusel Topping

1½ sticks (12 tablespoons) unsalted butter

2 cups light or dark brown sugar

1¼ cup unbleached flour

3 tablespoons ground cinnamon

Pinch of salt

✳

Preheat the oven to 350°. Butter and flour a rectangular coffee cake pan.

In a mixing bowl, cream the butter, sugar, and zest together. Add the eggs one at a time, mixing them completely into the batter after each addition.

Sift the dry ingredients together. Add the dry ingredients alternately with the sour cream to the batter. Stir in the vanilla extract. If fruit is desired, gently fold the fruit into the batter.

Pour the batter into the prepared pan and sprinkle the Streusel Topping evenly over the batter. Bake for 55 to 60 minutes or until a toothpick inserted in the center comes out clean.

## For the Streusel Topping

In a food processor or with a pastry blender, cut all ingredients together until the mixture resembles coarse meal, about the size of peas. Top the coffee cake with the streusel topping.

You can make the streusel mixture crunchier by spreading it on a cookie sheet and baking for 5 to 8 minutes before sprinkling it on the cake batter.

*Serves 8 to 12.*

Okay, we admit this dish takes a little last minute preparation, but Kellie's father loved to cook these hash browns on Saturday mornings just before the first college game, so it's a sentimental favorite. Boil the potatoes the night before and fry them up at halftime. Serve with Baked Eggs and fresh fruit.

# RJ's Hash Browns

4 baking potatoes, peeled and quartered
4 tablespoons butter
1 small onion, chopped
½ teaspoon Season-All seasoning salt

＊

Put the peeled and quartered potatoes in a pan of salted water. Bring to a boil and cook for 6 to 8 minutes or until a paring knife just pierces the potato. Don't overcook them, or they disintegrate when frying.

Drain the potatoes and lay them out on a cutting board. As they cool, dice the potatoes.

In a large, heavy skillet melt the butter over medium-high. When the butter starts to bubble, add the onion and sauté for 2 to 3 minutes or until the onion just begins to soften.

Add the potatoes, tossing to coat in the butter. Leave the potatoes to brown for 2 to 3 minutes. Don't keep stirring or they won't brown properly. Fry the potatoes, turning occasionally with a metal spatula for 15 to 18 minutes or until nicely brown and crusty. Add the seasoning salt about halfway through the frying process.

Serve the potatoes immediately, or spread on a cookie sheet and keep warm in the oven on low heat for up to 20 minutes.

*Serves 4.*

> "They're big. They're strong. They're fast. Their mothers love them . . . and they'll kill you."
>
> Jim Walden, Iowa State Coach on the Nebraska Cornhuskers

The apple cider and brown sugar in this dish combine to glaze the sausage and apples, and it's just delicious. Team up with scrambled eggs and coffee cake, and you've got the makings of the perfect day of Sunday football.

---

## Glazed Sausage and Apples

2 pounds small breakfast sausage links
¼ cup brown sugar
2 Granny Smith apples, peeled, cored and sliced
⅓ cup apple cider
1 large onion, very thinly sliced

*

In a large skillet over medium-high heat, brown the sausages; remove and drain on paper towels. Pour off the drippings from the pan.

In a medium bowl, combine the brown sugar, apples, apple cider, and onion slices. Sauté them in the skillet over medium-heat for 8 to 10 minutes.

Return the sausages to the pan and simmer until ready to serve. The glaze will thicken as it cooks and coat the sausages and apples.

*Serves 6 to 8.*

Typically bacon requires last minute attention as you fry it just before serving. This version lets you bake it up during the first half of the game. Serve with Cheese Strata and some fruit.

---

# Glazed Bacon

1 pound bacon
1 cup brown sugar

\*

Preheat oven to 300°. Bring bacon to room temperature. Line a baking sheet with aluminum foil.

Cut bacon strips in half lengthwise and separate bacon into individual strips.

Place bacon strips one at a time in brown sugar and press so that the bacon is coated on each side. Carefully place coated bacon strips side by side on a cooling rack and place the rack on the aluminum-lined baking sheet.

Bake for about 1 hour or until crisp.

Remove from oven and, using tongs, remove glazed bacon from rack and place on a piece of parchment paper. The bacon will harden as it cools. Serve at room temperature.

*Serves 4 to 6.*

> The Second World War so severely depleted the ranks of the football league that, in 1943, the Philadelphia Eagles and the Pittsburgh Steelers were forced to combine their teams for the season. The conjoined team had two coaches: Greasy Neale from the Eagles and Walt Keislung from the Steelers. The team was known as both the Phil-Pitts and the Steagles. To the relief of the players—and, we're sure, the coaches—the teams returned to normal the following season.

# Halftime Extravaganzas

## Main Dishes for the Hungriest Fans

America's game features a cast of characters who bring the game to life. Over the years, we've been entertained by the antics, theatrics, athletic performance, and sideline dramatics of players, coaches, commentators, and even fellow fans. Here are a few of our favorites.

While the media certainly spotlights some of the more colorful personalities, we've always had our fair share of eccentrics. Nicknamed football's "Magnificent Misfit," fullback Joe Don Looney played for four teams between 1964 and 1969 and was famous for being a coach's nightmare. He refused to practice because he said he already knew the plays and ignored his blockers because, according to Joe Don, "A good back makes his own holes. Anyone can run where the holes are."

And don't think the coaching staff is exempt. When we think coaches, we typically recall Vince Lombardi's intensity and the unflappable Tom Landry—but we've also enjoyed Jerry Granville, former coach of the Houston Oilers and the Atlanta Falcons. Granville is famous for leaving tickets at Will Call for deceased celebrities, including Buddy Holly, James Dean, and Elvis.

Then there's Bevo. The Texas Longhorns' mascot has had a long and colorful career with the team since the steer's introduction in 1916. Bevo I was served as an entrée at a postseason banquet. Bevo II—vowing revenge—charged an SMU cheerleader, who fended him off with a megaphone. Bevo III terrorized the Texas campus after escaping from his pen, and Bevo IV took on the Baylor band when offended by their rendition of "America the Beautiful."

The fans also get some credit for the game's eccentricity. In November 1896, the Georgia Tech team arrived by train in Auburn to play their archrivals. Hoping for a home team advantage, Auburn fans greased the tracks and watched as the train skidded past the station for five miles. They were a determined bunch, the Auburn fans. Georgia Tech players were forced to hike back to the station with all their equipment, and then suit up for the game. The exhausted Yellow Jackets were defeated 45–0.

College pranksters? Maybe so, but professional teams have their fair share of fanatical fans. In 1958, during Vince Lombardi's first season coaching Green Bay, a dedicated Packers fan spiked the opposing Forty-Niners' water bucket with vodka. The tipsy Forty-Niners went on to win 33–12.

The characters who love the game keep things colorful and entertaining, both on and off the field. This chapter features main dishes that have rich, unique qualities about them. Solid performers that are easy to prepare and that work around commercial breaks, they bring something special to your football parties. Use them as a guideline to create your own individual version—something that sets you apart.

This dish is truly addictive. You can also make the chicken on the grill, slice it into strips and pour the sauce on top. Serve this individually or on a platter, so that everyone gets the taste of the hot chicken with the cool refreshing salad.

---

# Buffalo Chicken Salad

1 cup Maili's Blue Cheese Dressing (or dressing of your choice)
2 heads of romaine lettuce, chopped
6 stalks of celery, chopped
4 boneless, skinless chicken breasts (1½–2 pounds)
¼ teaspoon salt, plus more for seasoning
2 tablespoons flour
2 tablespoons canola oil
4 tablespoons butter
⅓ cup Frank's Hot Sauce (or the hot sauce of your choice)

## Maili's Blue Cheese Dressing

2 stalks celery, chopped (about 1 cup)
1 tablespoon yellow onion, chopped
8 ounces blue cheese, crumbled (reserve about ¼ cup to add in at the end)
½ cup mayonnaise
½ cup sour cream
¾ cup buttermilk (can substitute milk)
2 tablespoons rice wine vinegar or mild white vinegar
1 teaspoon of your favorite hot sauce
1 tablespoon Worcestershire sauce
Freshly ground pepper to taste

*

To make the dressing, put the celery and onion in a food processor. Puree until vegetables are finely chopped.

Add the remaining ingredients, except the ¼ cup of reserved blue cheese, and process until smooth. Pour into a serving container and add the reserved blue cheese crumbles.

If you like the dressing creamy smooth, put all the cheese in the food processor at once.

In a large bowl, combine the lettuce, celery, and blue cheese dressing and set aside.

Cut the chicken into strips and season with salt. Combine the ¼ teaspoon salt with the flour and sprinkle salted flour on chicken strips.

In a very small saucepan, combine the butter and hot sauce. Cook over low heat and mix well.

Heat the canola oil in a large frying pan over medium-high heat. It is *very* important that the pan is hot before you add the chicken. Add the chicken and cook until nicely browned, about 2 to 3 minutes per side. Pour hot sauce mixture over the chicken and stir to coat chicken completely.

Put salad on individual plates or one large platter. Top with hot chicken. Serve immediately. It is best served hot, but we've been known to eat all the cold leftovers the next day.

*Serves 4.*

Easily transported to tailgates, or turned into a sandwich for the *Monday Night Football* game, this recipe effortlessly doubles or triples for a big crowd. It's a great way to use up leftover roast chicken, or you can simply buy a roast chicken from the deli.

---

## Dried Cranberry and Pecan Chicken Salad

2–3 cups shredded chicken
1 cup celery, chopped
¾ cup dried cranberries (or substitute dried cherries or raisins)
1 small apple, unpeeled, chopped
1 cup pecans, roasted and roughly chopped
¼ cup mayonnaise
1½ tablespoons coarse ground mustard
¼ teaspoon salt
¼ teaspoon freshly ground black pepper
Juice of one fresh lemon, optional

Combine all ingredients in a large bowl and mix well. Let sit a few minutes before serving, and then taste to see if you prefer more mayonnaise, salt, or pepper. We usually sneak a few extra dried cranberries in because we love them.

Serve the salad on a bed of Boston lettuce or with the bread of your choice for sandwiches.

*Serves 5 to 7.*

*

*Note*: Raw nuts don't impart nearly as much flavor as roasted nuts. Place the pecans on a cookies sheet and roast in a preheated 350° oven for 8 to 12 minutes. Watch carefully, as nuts burn easily.

> Fans can sometimes be so vocal and enthusiastic that it's hard for the snapper to hear the "hike" call. When the quarterback is working out of the shotgun and lined up a few feet behind the center, he will lift his foot up, put it back down, and then the players all count in their heads so that they're in sync.

This recipe calls for Panko Japanese bread crumbs, which are lighter, larger, and flakier than regular breadcrumbs. They've become easier to find in local grocery stores, but if you have trouble locating them, substitute fresh breadcrumbs. The dish goes together during the pregame festivities and is ready by halftime.

# Cornmeal Crusted Chicken

6–8 boneless skinless chicken breasts

3 cups buttermilk

2 tablespoons hot sauce of your choice

1 cup flour

2 cups cornmeal

3 cups Panko (Japanese bread crumbs)

2 tablespoons cornstarch, optional

1 tablespoon kosher salt

1 teaspoon freshly ground pepper

2 sticks (1 cup) butter

\*

Combine buttermilk and hot sauce in a large bowl. Soak the chicken in buttermilk up to a day in advance in the refrigerator or for as little as 10 minutes.

Preheat the oven to 400° and line a baking sheet with heavy-duty aluminum foil or parchment paper. Melt the butter in a pan, making sure the pan is large enough for dipping the chicken in the melted butter.

Combine flour, cornmeal, Panko, cornstarch, salt, and pepper in a bowl. Then divide the mixture in half between the two shallow dishes (cake pans work well). Dip the chicken in the cornmeal mixture, then the melted butter, and finally the second cornmeal mixture. Gently shake off the excess and place crusted chicken on the lined baking sheet.

Bake for 45 to 55 minutes or until chicken is golden brown.

*Serves 6 to 8.*

Developed as a special request for one of Maili's events, this recipe has quickly become a game day favorite. Long-handled tongs are handy for this dish.

---

# Maili's Buttermilk Fried Chicken

2 whole chickens or precut chicken parts

## Soaking mixture

8 cups buttermilk (½ gallon)
2 eggs, slightly beaten
3 tablespoons kosher salt
1 teaspoon freshly ground black pepper
¼ cup Frank's Hot Sauce (or sauce of your choice)

## Flour dredging mixture

1½ cups unbleached all-purpose flour
3 tablespoons kosher salt
1 tablespoon cayenne pepper
1 tablespoon chili powder
1 tablespoon cornstarch
1 tablespoon freshly ground black pepper
1 tablespoon Coleman's dried mustard, optional
7 ounce bag Panko (Japanese bread crumbs)

*

Shortening or oil for frying

*

Preheat oven to 375°. Line a cookie sheet with paper grocery bags.

If using whole chicken, cut into 8 to 10 pieces. Rinse and pat chicken pieces dry.

In a very large bowl, combine the soaking mixture ingredients. Add the chicken pieces and soak at least one hour at room temperature or overnight in the refrigerator.

In a very large frying pan or deep Dutch oven, pour in enough oil or shortening (or a combination of the two) to fill the pan to a depth of about 1 inch. Heat the oil to 350°.

Combine the flour dredging mixture. Dredge the chicken in flour mixture and set aside.

Cook chicken in hot oil a few pieces at a time. Putting in too many at once reduces the temperature of the oil and the chicken won't crisp. Fry until golden brown. When done, place chicken pieces on the paper-lined cookie sheet. The paper bag absorbs excess oil.

Serve immediately or cool and refrigerate. To reheat the chicken, place on a cooling rack on top of a cookie sheet. Place in preheated 375° oven for 20 minutes.

*Serves 8.*

"I have seen women walk right past a TV set with a football game on and—this always amazes me—not stop to watch, even if the TV is showing replays of what we call a 'good hit,' which is a tackle that causes at least one major internal organ to actually fly out of a player's body."

Dave Barry

Instead of a traditional white sauce with flour filler, this recipe is cheese, cheese, and more cheese with some macaroni thrown in. We like to use Pecorino Romano cheese, but the dish works with Parmesan, which you can buy grated. Serve with a green salad and red wine.

---

# Midfield Mac and Cheese

1 pound large elbow macaroni, or pasta of your choice
1 cup heavy cream or half-and-half
6 cups sharp cheddar cheese, grated
1½ cups Pecorino Romano or Parmesan cheese, freshly grated
1 8-ounce package cream cheese
1–2 tablespoons hot sauce

      &#42;

Preheat oven to 375º.

In a 6- to 8-quart saucepan, cook the pasta in salted water until al dente. Rinse the macaroni in cold water until completely cool. Set aside in a large bowl.

Add the heavy cream, 4 cups grated cheddar cheese, and the Pecorino Romano to the pasta and mix thoroughly. Add the hot sauce and stir to combine.

Break the cream cheese into marble-sized pieces (it will be sticky). Try to keep the cream cheese pieces as separate as possible. Mix them into the macaroni. The other cheese may clump to the cream cheese, but don't worry, it will still taste great.

Spoon the macaroni and cheese mixture into a 9 × 13-inch baking dish with deep sides. Put the remaining two cups of grated cheddar cheese on top.

Bake for 30 minutes, or until the top is crisp and bubbly.

*Serves 8 to 10.*

This is one of our all-purpose sauces. We use it in lasagna, as a top-ping on our pizzas, and over fresh pasta for a quick Monday night game dinner. It freezes beautifully, so we always have some on hand.

# All-Pro Tomato-Meat Sauce

3 tablespoons olive oil

1 medium onion, finely chopped

1 carrot, finely chopped

1 celery stalk, finely chopped

½ pound ground beef

½ pound Italian sausage, hot or sweet, removed from the casing

2 28-ounce cans whole plum tomatoes, drained

3 cloves garlic, minced

1 bay leaf

1 teaspoon dried oregano

¼ teaspoon hot pepper flakes, optional

Salt and pepper to taste

3 tablespoons tomato paste

*

In a heavy skillet or Dutch oven, heat the oil over medium heat. Add the chopped onion, carrot, and celery and sauté until soft but not brown, about 8 minutes. Add the beef and the sausage and stir until the meat is no longer pink.

Add the tomatoes, garlic, bay leaf, oregano, hot pepper flakes, salt, and pepper. Bring to a simmer, cover, and con-tinue cooking, stirring occasionally, for 45 minutes. As you stir, break up the tomatoes.

Discard the bay leaf and stir in the tomato paste. Simmer, uncovered, for another 10 minutes or until thickened.

The sauce can be kept in the refrigerator, covered, for up to three days or frozen, in an airtight container, for two months.

*Makes 4 cups.*

> George Halas began coaching the "Monsters of the Midway" in 1920, the same year the NFL was launched. He guided the team for 40 years, still the longest tenure in league history.

Lasagna is one of those classic comfort foods. It always satisfies and appeals to everyone. You can assemble the lasagna the night before a game and pop it in the oven before kick-off. Serve with green salad and our Balsamic Vinaigrette and Roasted Garlic Bread on the side.

# Lasagna

2 cups ricotta cheese
2 large egg yolks
½ cup grated Parmesan cheese
½ cup minced parsley
Nutmeg to taste
Salt and freshly ground pepper to taste
12 ounces dried lasagna noodles
4 cups All-Pro Tomato-Meat Sauce
1 pound Italian Fontina cheese, grated
⅓ cup grated Parmesan cheese

\*

Preheat the oven to 375°. Butter a 9 × 13-inch baking dish.

Mix the ricotta, egg yolks, Parmesan, parsley, nutmeg, salt, and pepper in a bowl. (This can be made a day ahead and refrigerated, covered.)

Bring a large pot of salted water to a boil. Add the lasagna noodles and cook, uncovered, about 8 minutes, stirring occasionally. Cook until flexible but not tender. Drain and rinse under cold water to prevent sticking. Dry the noodles between kitchen towels.

In the prepared dish, spread 1 cup of the All-Pro Tomato-Meat Sauce. Top with a layer of about one third of the lasagna noodles. Spread the ricotta cheese mixture on top of the noodles in an even layer. Top with another layer of noodles and cover with 1 cup All-Pro Meat Sauce. Sprinkle with 1½ cups Fontina cheese.

Top with one more layer of lasagna noodles and cover with the remaining meat sauce. Sprinkle evenly with the rest of the Fontina cheese and the Parmesan.

Bake for 35 to 45 minutes or until bubbly and lightly browned. Let stand for 10 minutes before cutting into squares.

*Serves 6 to 8.*

> "Good morning, Mr. Rentzel. It's 8:00 a.m. It's 15 below zero, and there's a 20-mile-per-hour wind coming out of the northwest. Have a nice day."
>
> Wake-up call to Dallas wide receiver Lance Rentzel on the morning of "The Ice Bowl"

This is a great *Monday Night Football* recipe, because with the ingredients on hand, it takes just minutes to put together and you can be enjoying dinner by the end of the first quarter. Serve with a glass of Chianti and a green salad.

# French Bread Pizza

1 large loaf French bread
2 cups All-Pro Tomato-Meat Sauce (or pizza sauce of your
    choice)
2 cups grated Mozzarella

\*

Preheat the oven to 375°.

Slice the French bread in half and then slice each half horizontally so that you have 4 pieces. Put the bread on a baking sheet.

Top each quarter with ½ cup of the tomato-meat sauce. Sprinkle ½ cup of the grated cheese over the sauce.

Bake for 20 to 25 minutes or until the cheese melts completely.

*Serves 4.*

We owe the tradition of a Thanksgiving Day game to the Detroit Lions. In July of 1930 George Richards was awarded a franchise in Ohio after three unsuccessful attempts to get one in Detroit. Richards purchased the Ohio Spartans and promptly moved them to Detroit, where they scheduled one of their first games on Thanksgiving. With the exception of a five-year break from 1939 to 1944, this tradition has been maintained ever since.

Double Team Shrimp is so named because friends and family love both sauces equally. The Classic Shrimp Cocktail Sauce works for traditionalists, and Triple Citrus Thai Chili Sauce is great for fans who want something new. If grilling is your game, thread the shrimp on skewers and cook on the grill.

## Double Team Shrimp

2 pounds large shrimp (16–20 count), peeled and deveined
3 tablespoons canola oil
1 teaspoon kosher salt
⅛ teaspoon fresh ground pepper
Classic Shrimp Cocktail Sauce (page 6)
Triple Citrus Thai Chili Sauce (page 7)
Cilantro or parsley for garnish, optional

*

Place shrimp in a large bowl and toss with 2 tablespoons oil, salt, and pepper.

Heat a large sauté pan to medium-high. Wait for pan to heat completely and then add remaining 1 tablespoon oil to the pan. Cook the shrimp for about 1 minute on each side or until they are bright pink. Cook the shrimp in batches so as not to overcrowd.

Remove the shrimp to a serving dish and serve with tooth-picks for spearing and the two dipping sauces on the side.

*Serves 4 to 6.*

Pulled pork can be used in a number of recipes. You can put it in burritos or quesadillas or make pulled pork barbecue sandwiches with our Quick Kick Barbecue Sauce. While it takes some time to cook, it's hassle free and can be made up to two days in advance and frozen for up to a month.

# Pigskin Pulled Pork

1 5- to 6-pound pork shoulder
3 tablespoons of your favorite hot sauce
1 teaspoon kosher salt

\*

Preheat oven to 375°.

Tear off 3 large lengths of heavy-duty aluminum foil. Place the foil opposite ways in a heavy duty roasting pan. Place the whole pork shoulder on top of the foil layers, fat side down. Rub hot sauce over pork evenly. Then sprinkle salt evenly over the pork. Wrap each layer of foil around the pork individually, tightly closing each one.

Place in oven and cook for 3½ to 4 hours. Remove from heat and let cool until you can pull it apart with your fingers. It should be so tender that it falls apart.

To reheat, heat 1 tablespoon vegetable oil over medium heat in a heavy saucepan and add the pulled pork. If you're planning on making pulled pork sandwiches, add the barbecue sauce of your choice.

*Serves 10 to 15.*

---

"Speed, strength and the inability to register pain immediately."

Reggie Williams commenting on his greatest strengths

While barbecue aficionados prefer slow cooking their ribs in a smoker, that's not practical for northerners during the play-offs in January. This recipe lets us enjoy tender, delicious ribs throughout the season. Serve with cold beer and Onion-Cheddar Corn Bread.

---

## Auntie Fran's Baby Back Ribs

2 racks of Baby Back Ribs (about 1 pound each)
Salt
2 cups of your favorite barbecue sauce (or use our Quick Kick Barbecue Sauce, page 51)

\*

Preheat oven to 400°.

Line a large baking sheet with aluminum foil. Place ribs on foil in a single layer. Lightly season the ribs with salt.

Bake for 20 minutes. Reduce oven temperature to 200° and baste the ribs with the barbecue sauce. Cook for an additional 2½ hours, basting every 30 minutes. If you prefer a thicker glaze, baste the ribs every 20 minutes, or 6 times total.

*Serves 4 to 6.*

This recipe is perfect for the Sunday night game as the season wears on, the temperature drops, and you want a deep, rich, flavorful dish that comforts. Serve with mashed potatoes or noodles and red wine.

# Braised Short Ribs

3 pounds boneless short ribs
2 teaspoons salt
2 teaspoons freshly ground black pepper
1 large onion, coarsely chopped
2 garlic cloves, chopped
1 cup dry red wine
2 teaspoons dry Italian herbs
1 14½-ounce can peeled and chopped tomatoes

*

Preheat the oven to 500°. Line a large baking sheet with foil.

Season the ribs generously with salt and freshly ground pepper. Arrange the ribs, fat side up, in a single layer on the prepared baking sheet. Roast until the ribs are golden brown, about 25 minutes. Remove the ribs from the oven and reduce the oven temperature to 325°.

Transfer the ribs to a large, heavy ovenproof pot or Dutch oven. Combine the remaining ingredients in a medium bowl and pour over the ribs. Roast uncovered at 325° for 2½ to 3 hours, until the meat is easily pulled off the bone with a fork. Taste the sauce, and season with salt and pepper if needed.

*Serves 6 to 8.*

# Bowl Food

## Soups, Stews, and Chilis

"Good morning, Mr. Rentzel. It's 8:00 a.m. It's 15 below zero, and there's a 20-mile-per-hour wind coming out of the northwest. Have a nice day." That was the wake-up call to Dallas wide receiver Lance Rentzel the morning of the 1967 NFL Championship Game between the Green Bay Packers and the Cowboys—true story. With a game-time temperature of 13 degrees below zero and a wind`chill factor of minus 46 degrees, it remains a mystery why the game was played at all. Yet 50,000 dedicated fans huddled together at Green Bay's Lambeau Field to watch their team defeat the Cowboys 21–17. Later dubbed "The Ice Bowl," the game is an NFL legend.

In November 1950, the Michigan Wolverines took on the Ohio State Buckeyes in what would later be called "The Snow Bowl." Playing in blizzard conditions, the two teams punted a total of 45 times and accomplished only 68 total offensive yards between them. Michigan won the game 9–3, despite never managing a first down and failing all nine pass attempts.

While both these foul weather games became part of football lore, neither was quite as comical as the December 1988 playoff fiasco between the Bears and the Eagles. Playing in Chicago's infamous Soldier Field Stadium, Bears quarterback Mike Tomczak and Randall Cunningham of the Eagles skillfully led their teams through the first quarter and into the second, with each team scoring. Then Mother Nature decided to step in and make things more interesting. The Bears were up 17–6 midway through the second quarter when a dense gray fog descended on the field.

For the rest of the game, stadium fans had no idea what was going on, and television viewers were completely out of luck. CBS analyst Terry Bradshaw couldn't even see enough to call the game! Despite Cunningham's 407-yard passing effort, the Bears won the game 20–12. Center Jay Hilgenberg told the *Philadelphia Tribune*, "We were all relieved. With the fog, there won't be any films for the coaches to grade." It was quickly dubbed—you guessed it—"The Fog Bowl."

Inclement weather is just part of the game. As the season wears on and fall gives way to winter, these are the recipes we turn to for comfort and warmth. Hearty, satisfying, and infused with deep, rich flavors, these dishes actually improve overnight in the refrigerator. Anything that gets prepared the day before a game and slowly reheated while we're watching the action deserves a place of honor in our kitchen. Serve them up with bread and cheese during commercial breaks, and say a prayer that your team is still a playoff contender.

Echoing our favorite fall flavors—apples, cider, and butternut squash—this soup never fails to get compliments at tailgate events. Leftovers can be served for *Monday Night Football* with bread and a cheese platter.

---

# Butternut Squash and Apple Soup

5 tablespoons butter

2½ pounds butternut squash, peeled, seeded and cut in ½" pieces

1 medium onion, diced

½ cup carrots, peeled and chopped

2 Granny Smith apples, peeled, cored and chopped

5 cups chicken stock

1 cup apple cider

1 tablespoon brown sugar

½ teaspoon salt

½ teaspoon ground cinnamon

¼ cup heavy cream

*

In a large pot, melt the butter over medium-high heat. Add the squash, onion, and carrot; sauté until softened, about 15 minutes.

Add the apples, chicken stock, and cider and bring to a boil. Reduce the heat, cover, and simmer until the vegetables are tender, stirring occasionally, about 30 minutes.

Remove from the heat and, working in batches, puree the soup in a blender. Return the soup to the pot and stir in the brown sugar, salt, cinnamon, and heavy cream.

Slowly reheat the soup on medium-low. Ladle the soup into bowls.

*Serves 6 to 8.*

This soup has all the deep and comforting flavors of our favorite chili, but it travels well in a wide-mouth thermos to tailgate parties. Serve with grilled corn muffins, and this will see you through even the coldest of Homecoming games.

# Chili Chaser Soup

1 pound ground beef
1 onion, chopped
2 garlic cloves, peeled and chopped
1 29-ounce can pureed tomatoes
4 cups beef stock
1 15½-ounce can black beans, drained
1 chipotle chili in adobo sauce, chopped
1 teaspoon salt
Sharp cheddar cheese, grated
Cilantro, chopped
Sour cream

*

Brown the beef in a 5-quart saucepan. Drain fat. Add the onions and garlic and sauté the vegetables until soft, about 5 minutes.

Add the next five ingredients. Cover and simmer for 35 to 45 minutes, stirring occasionally. Serve with cheddar cheese, cilantro, and sour cream as toppings.

*Serves 6 to 8.*

"The pads don't keep you from getting hurt. They just keep you from getting killed."

Defensive end Chad Bratzke

The British brought this soup home from India, where it was originally called *milakutanni* or "pepper-water." We like this curry-inspired soup because it's warm and comforting and makes the perfect meal as cold weather sets in and the playoffs are imminent. Serve with warm bread and a green salad.

# Mulligatawny

4 tablespoons butter
2 celery stalks, diced
2 large onions, chopped
2 medium carrots, diced
1 green pepper, diced
2 cloves garlic, minced
1 tablespoon curry powder
¼ teaspoon ground cumin
¼ teaspoon ground cloves
Dash cayenne pepper
Salt and pepper to taste
8 cups chicken broth
3 cups cooked chicken, chopped
1 14-ounce can whole tomatoes, chopped
2 tart apples, peeled, cored and diced
2 tablespoons minced parsley

Melt the butter over medium heat in a large stock pot. Sauté the celery, onion, carrots, green pepper, and garlic until the vegetables are soft, about 5 minutes.

Add the curry powder, cumin, clove, cayenne, salt, pepper, chicken stock, chicken, tomatoes, apples, and parsley. Reduce the heat and simmer, covered, for about 30 minutes.

*Serves 4 to 6.*

**"Looks like we're making some progress."**

Tom Landry, after a 31–31 tie against the Giants, halting a 10-game losing streak

Beer is the secret ingredient to this quick and easy comfort food. Serve with one of our sandwiches for a great *Monday Night Football* dinner or with Coin Toss Cheese Crisps for a light lunch during the afternoon game.

---

# Touchdown Tomato Soup

½ medium yellow onion, peeled and quartered

3 cloves garlic, peeled

2 28-ounce cans diced tomatoes

¼ cup fresh basil leaves (1 teaspoon dried)

1 teaspoon fresh thyme leaves (¼ teaspoon dried)

¼ teaspoon red pepper flakes

½ teaspoon salt, or more to taste

Ground pepper to taste

1 tablespoon olive oil

2 cups chicken broth

¼ cup beer

✳

Put onion, garlic, one can of the tomatoes, basil leaves, thyme leaves, red pepper flakes, salt, and pepper in a blender. Process until onion, garlic, and leaves are completely chopped and mixed in.

Heat 1 tablespoon olive oil in a large soup pot over medium heat. Pour the blended soup mixture into the pot. Reduce the heat and stir.

Puree the second can of diced tomatoes in the blender and add to the soup pot. Add chicken broth and beer and heat through before serving.

*Serves 4.*

**"I think it's a good idea."**

John McKay, Buccaneers coach, when asked by a reporter what he thought of his team's execution

The perfect complement to a snowy weekend game, this chowder is a staple for New England fans. It's important that you add the salt when cooking the potatoes, as they will not absorb the flavor after they are cooked, and the dish will be bland. Serve with warm French bread and a green salad.

# Classic New England Clam Chowder

6 slices bacon, chopped
1 medium yellow onion, chopped
2 stalks celery, chopped
2 tablespoons flour
1–2 tablespoons butter, optional
4 cups whole milk or half-and-half
2 teaspoons salt
2 pounds potatoes (about 5 medium potatoes), peeled and
    chopped
3 6.5-ounce cans of chopped clams with juice
1 teaspoon Tabasco sauce
2 teaspoons Pickapeppa or Worcestershire sauce, optional
1 tablespoon dry sherry, optional

✳

In a large, heavy stock pot over medium-high heat, cook bacon until crisp, about 4 to 6 minutes. Add the onion and sauté in bacon fat until translucent and soft, about 5 minutes. Sprinkle onions with a pinch of salt, then add celery and sauté for an additional 5 minutes.

Lower the heat and sprinkle the flour over the mixture. Add butter if desired. Stirring constantly over low heat, cook flour and vegetables for 2 minutes.

Add milk, salt and potatoes. Cook for 15 minutes over medium heat, or until potatoes are tender.

Stir in the clams and their juice, then add Tabasco, Pickapeppa or Worcestershire sauce, and sherry. Add freshly ground pepper to taste and serve.

*Serves 4.*

This is a traditional fish stew with deep ties to the San Francisco Bay area. We like to serve it during college bowl games with sourdough bread and a light red wine.

# Fisherman's Wharf Cioppino

½ cup olive oil
1 large yellow onion, chopped
1 cup chopped parsley leaves
2 cloves garlic, chopped
1 35-ounce can plum tomatoes, broken up with a spoon
1 8-ounce can tomato sauce
1 bay leaf
½ teaspoon dried oregano
½ teaspoon dried basil
Salt and freshly ground pepper to taste
1 teaspoon red pepper flakes, optional
1 cup dry white wine
½ pound shrimp, shelled, deveined
¾ pound cod (or other firm white fish), skinned, boned and cut into 1" cubes
1 pound cooked crab claws, cut into 3" pieces
½ pound mussels, beards scrubbed off
½ pound steamer clams

　　✳

In a large skillet or Dutch oven, heat the oil over medium-high heat. Sauté the onion, parsley, and garlic until lightly browned and soft, about 10 minutes.

Add the tomatoes, tomato sauce, bay leaf, oregano, basil, salt, pepper, and if desired, red pepper to taste. Cover and simmer gently for 1 hour. (This can be prepared one day ahead and refrigerated, stored in an airtight container.)

Add the wine, shrimp, and white fish. Simmer for 10 minutes. Add the crab pieces, mussels, and clams. Check the seasoning and continue simmering for an additional 8 minutes or until the steamers have opened.

Serve in large soup bowls.

*Serves 4 to 6.*

The NFL draft is an annual two-day event, held in late April in New York City. The draft consists of seven rounds. Each team has one pick per round. The team holding the worst record from the prior season picks first, that with the second-worst record picks second, and so on, until the Super Bowl winners make the final pick in each round. Each team has 15 minutes to make their pick in the first round and only 5 minutes for each additional round.

This is the quintessential fall dish complete with slow-cooked chicken, apple cider, and cinnamon stewed together and finished off with cream. Serve this during the Sunday evening game with rice pilaf and a green salad.

# Cider-Stewed Chicken

3 pounds chicken pieces (breasts, legs, thighs)
Salt
Freshly ground pepper
¼ cup plus 2 tablespoons flour
2 tablespoons butter
1 tablespoon olive oil
2 shallots, minced
1½ cups apple cider
½ cup dry white wine
1 teaspoon fresh thyme (½ teaspoon dried)
1 cinnamon stick
1 bay leaf
1 cup chicken stock
2 teaspoons apple cider vinegar
¼ cup heavy cream
Salt and pepper to taste

\*

Remove any excess fat from the chicken. Sprinkle with salt and pepper to taste and dredge in ¼ cup of flour until coated.

In a large skillet or Dutch oven, melt the butter and oil over medium heat. Add the chicken in batches and sauté, turning occasionally, until the chicken is golden brown, about 10 minutes per batch. Remove the chicken to a platter and pour off all but 1 tablespoon of the fat from the pan.

Add the shallots to the pan and sauté over medium heat until they are softened, about 2 minutes. Pour the cider and wine into the pan and bring to a boil, scraping up any brown bits from the bottom. Add the thyme, cinnamon stick, and bay leaf and boil for 5 minutes.

Add the chicken stock, vinegar, salt and pepper to taste. Return the chicken to the pan, cover, and simmer over low heat for 30 minutes.

Remove the chicken to a platter, cover, and keep warm. Remove the cinnamon stick and bay leaf and discard. Combine the reserved 2 tablespoons of flour with 2 tablespoons of water and mix until smooth. Add to the cider sauce and boil over high heat for 5 minutes or until thickened. Stir in the cream and season with salt and pepper to taste.

Return the chicken to the sauce, heat through, and serve.

*Serves 4 to 6.*

---

**"I don't know why they scheduled this game here—I guess because the top of Mt. Everest was booked."**

*Los Angeles Times* columnist Jim Murray on "The Ice Bowl"

Kellie's father was a lifelong Nebraska Cornhuskers fan, and every time they played their archrival—the Oklahoma Sooners—this family favorite was served. The dish gets its name from the street where they lived when Kellie's mom developed the recipe. The secret to its special flavor is the cinnamon. This chili doubles easily and freezes well. Serve with cornbread and the toppings of your choice.

# Liberty Street Chili

2 pounds ground beef
1 medium onion, chopped
1 1.25-ounce package chili seasoning mix
1 28-ounce can whole tomatoes, with juice
1 13-ounce jar chunky salsa
1 teaspoon ground cumin
1 teaspoon ground coriander
Salt and freshly ground pepper to taste
¼ teaspoon ground cinnamon
Pinch of dried chipotle chili powder, optional
2–3 15-ounce cans red kidney beans, drained

*

In a Dutch oven, brown the meat over medium-high heat and drain the fat. Add the onion and chili mix. (Add 1 cup water if you want a thinner consistency.) Add the whole tomatoes, including the juice, salsa, cumin, coriander, salt, pepper, cinnamon, and chipotle chili powder.

Simmer for 1 to 2 hours or until the flavors have a chance to mingle and the onion is tender. As the chili cooks, separate and crush the tomatoes with a spoon. (The dish can be made to this point two days ahead. Cover and refrigerate.)

Add the kidney beans and heat through. Start with 2 cans of beans and add another if preferred.

Serve in large bowls and offer toppings including chopped fresh red onions, grated cheddar cheese, salsa, chopped fresh cilantro, and sour cream.

*Serves 6 to 8.*

There is nothing quite like a bowl of chili and a cold beer at the height of the season when the Wild Card spot is up for grabs. This traditional Texas chili can be made with or without beans, depending on your preference. Serve with cornbread and icy cold beer.

## Texas Beef Chili

¼ cup vegetable oil
3 pounds beef chuck or round, cut into ½" cubes
1 onion, chopped
4 cloves garlic, chopped
5 tablespoons chili powder
1 tablespoon ground cumin
1 tablespoon paprika
1 teaspoon dried Mexican oregano
1 teaspoon salt
1 8-ounce can tomato sauce
1 cup beef stock
1 chipotle in adobo sauce, chopped
2 cans kidney beans, optional

    ✻

In a large pot or Dutch oven, heat the oil over medium-high heat and cook the beef in batches until browned, about 6 minutes per batch. Add the onion and garlic and continue cooking about 5 minutes, or until vegetables are softened.

Add the chili powder, cumin, paprika, oregano, and salt and stir for an additional 2 minutes. Add the tomato sauce, beef stock, and chipotle.

Bring to a boil, cover, and simmer on low heat for 2 hours, stirring occasionally. If chili gets too thick, add some water ½ cup at a time.

Add the kidney beans if desired and heat through, then serve in bowls with chopped onion and grated cheese as toppings.

*Serves 6 to 8.*

This recipe comes from a sorority sister inclined to root for a distinctly inferior team, but we love the recipe just the same. It's a great dish for a playoff game because you can make it a day ahead and reheat it during the second quarter. Serve with Corn Soufflé and a green salad with vinaigrette.

# Pork Picadillo

2 tablespoons butter
2 tablespoons vegetable oil
1 large onion, finely chopped
3½ pounds boneless pork shoulder, cut in ¾" cubes
2 cloves garlic, minced
2 8-ounce cans tomato sauce
½ cup tomato-based chili sauce
1 teaspoon ground cinnamon
2 teaspoons salt
2 teaspoons ground cumin
½ cup dried currants
3 tablespoons vinegar
3 tablespoons brown sugar
2 green onions, thinly sliced
2 limes, cut into wedges
2 avocados, peeled and diced

*

Using a large Dutch oven, melt 1 tablespoon of butter with 1 tablespoon vegetable oil and sauté the onion until softened, about 5 minutes. Remove the onion and reserve. Add the remaining 1 tablespoon each of butter and vegetable oil to the pan and brown the meat in several batches.

Return the onions to the Dutch oven. Add the garlic, tomato sauce, chili sauce, cinnamon, salt, cumin, currants, vinegar, and brown sugar. Stir, cover, and simmer 45 minutes, or until the meat is tender, stirring occasionally and adding a little water if the sauce gets too thick.

Serve the Picadillo in a soup tureen or large decorative bowl, garnished with thinly sliced green onions, with the lime wedges and avocado on the side. Traditionally, guests ladle the Picadillo over the diced avocado and squeeze the lime juice over the top.

*Serves 8 to 10.*

The first professional football players to sport an insignia on their helmets were the 1950 Los Angeles Rams, who hand-painted yellow horns on their blue leather helmets.

According to Mark Twain, "New Orleans food is as delicious as the less criminal forms of sin." This dish—our tribute to the southern tier teams—can be made in advance up to the point of adding the shrimp. Then reheat it and add the shellfish at the last minute. The trick is to cook the vegetables so briefly that they stay crunchy and add texture to the dish.

# Shrimp Creole

¼ cup olive oil
3 cloves garlic, minced
1 cup green bell pepper, diced
1 cup red bell pepper, diced
1 cup celery, diced
8–10 plum tomatoes, diced
¼ teaspoon dried basil
½ teaspoon Italian herb seasoning
¼ teaspoon dried oregano
¼ teaspoon Old Bay seasoning
⅛ teaspoon Creole seasoning
Pinch cayenne pepper, optional
Chicken stock, optional
2 pounds shrimp, shelled and deveined
3 tablespoons fresh flat leaf parsley, minced
Salt and pepper to taste

＊

In a heavy pot, lightly brown the garlic in oil over medium heat. Add the tomatoes and cook until they begin to soften, about 2 minutes. Add the bell pepper, celery, and seasonings and cook for an additional 4 minutes.

Add the shrimp, cooking gently until they turn pink, 3 to 5 minutes. If the Creole appears too thick, thin with some chicken stock. Add parsley, season with salt and pepper, and adjust the seasonings as desired. Serve over rice.

*Serves 6.*

# Sideline Players
## Beans to Breads, Pasta to Potatoes

Elected NFL Commissioner in 1960, Pete Rozelle was a polished public relations man who knew how to sell football to the American people. His skillful negotiation with television network executives provided franchise owners with lucrative telecast rights and secured record prosperity for the league throughout the '60s.

But for Rozelle, daytime television wasn't enough. He was convinced he could bring pro football to prime time and further expand the fan base. An early bid to televise Friday night games was defeated, however, because critics feared the telecasts would damage high school game attendance.

Undeterred, Rozelle signed a deal with CBS in '66 and '67 to broadcast one Monday night game each year in prime time. These early experiments proved successful, but the network was still reluctant to sign on for more. So in 1970 Rozelle went to ABC—the lowest-ranking network at the time—and the rest is broadcast history.

Producer Roone Arledge hired controversial New York sports broadcaster Howard Cosell as a commentator, along with play-by-play man Keith Jackson. Arledge also wanted Frank Gifford on the team, but the seven-time Pro Bowl veteran was still under contract to CBS. Gifford recommended former Dallas Cowboys quarterback Don Meredith, and on September 21, 1970, "Dandy Don," Cosell, and Jackson took to the booth and launched a phenomenon that changed football season Monday nights forever.

*Monday Night Football* aired 555 Monday night games on ABC from 1970 to 2005 and still ranks as the second longest running prime time show in American television history. Across the country Monday night movie attendance dropped, and bowling leagues shifted to Tuesday nights as the show gained a solid fan base. In 1985 market share for the Miami vs. Chicago matchup was an unprecedented 46 percent!

During the show's run, colorful commentary and play-by-play action were provided by Fran Tarkenton, Alex Karras, Frank Gifford, OJ Simpson, Boomer Esiason, Joe Namath, Al Michaels, John Madden, and even Dennis Miller. The show also introduced eager fans to cutting-edge television technology, including slow motion replays, computerized graphics, and multi-angle play action made possible by the additional cameras ABC employed to capture the game.

Over three decades, the cast of characters who brought us *Monday Night Football* on ABC gave fans a new understanding and love of the game. They brought us onto the sidelines and up to the line of scrimmage, enriching our appreciation of the action on the field and the men who played the game.

We hope our side dishes offer the same qualities. Designed to support our main dishes, they offer guests some color, delicious flavors, and satisfying ways to complete the menu. These recipes complement the gridiron action with their easy and advance preparation so that the game is always in the spotlight.

Searching for something a little more exciting than baked beans, we developed this recipe and knew we had a winner. The best part is that you can assemble this dish the night before the game and put it in the oven just before kick-off. It's ready by halftime.

## Texas Baked Beans

½ pound bacon
1 medium onion, chopped
½ cup tomato-based chili sauce
3 tablespoons brown sugar
1 tablespoon apple cider vinegar
1 teaspoon salt
1 teaspoon dry mustard
Pinch of cayenne pepper
2 16-ounce cans pork and beans
1 16-ounce can kidney beans, drained

✻

Preheat oven to 350°.

In a heavy skillet, cook the bacon over medium heat until crisp, about 6 minutes. Transfer the bacon to a plate lined with paper towels. Sauté the onion in the bacon drippings until translucent, about 5 minutes.

In a medium bowl, stir together the chili sauce, brown sugar, vinegar, salt, dry mustard, and cayenne pepper. Add the sautéed onions and stir. Crumble the bacon into the mixture and add the beans.

Pour into a 9 × 13-inch pan and bake for 35 to 45 minutes or until bubbly.

*Serves 8 to 10.*

We love soup for cold, snowy days, and it pairs perfectly with our Cheddar Cheese Toasts. They're the ideal crunchy accompaniment and easy to make. The topping can be assembled in advance and kept refrigerated until you're ready to broil them.

# Cheddar Cheese Toasts

1 cup grated cheddar cheese
⅓ cup mayonnaise
1 clove garlic, minced
½ teaspoon dried thyme
½ teaspoon dried oregano
Pinch of salt and pepper
1 baguette, cut in ½" slices

✳

Preheat the broiler.

In a medium mixing bowl, combine the cheese, mayonnaise, garlic, herbs, salt, and pepper.

On a baking sheet, arrange the bread slices in a single layer and spread a teaspoon or two of the cheese mixture on the slices. Broil for 3 to 4 minutes or until the cheese is melted and lightly browned. Serve immediately.

*Makes 18 to 24 toasts.*

"A man who has no fear belongs in a mental institution . . . or on special teams."

New York Jets coach Walt Michaels

Biscuits are a great complement to soups and stews and can be made the morning of the game and gently reheated. Our version uses the food processor to cut in the butter, which saves time.

# Cheese Biscuits

2 cups flour
4 teaspoons baking powder
½ teaspoon cream of tartar
1 teaspoon granulated sugar
½ teaspoon salt
1 stick cold butter, cubed
⅔ cup milk
1 cup sharp cheddar cheese

*

Preheat the oven to 450°.

Sift together the flour, baking powder, cream of tartar, sugar, and salt. Put dry ingredients in a food processor, add the butter, and pulse briefly until the mixture resembles coarse crumbs.

In a large bowl, combine the flour/butter base with the milk and cheese and stir just until the dough starts to form a ball. Turn out onto a lightly floured surface and knead 8 to 10 times. Roll the dough out to a ½-inch thickness and cut into rounds with a biscuit cutter or a glass.

Bake on an ungreased cookie sheet for 10 to 12 minutes or until risen and golden brown.

*Makes 6 to 8 biscuits.*

The name "soufflé" can strike fear into the hearts of even the most seasoned of cooks, but this version doesn't require careful handling of egg whites or tiptoeing around the kitchen while it's baking. Ours is easily prepared early in the day and popped into the oven at halftime. We serve this with grilled dishes or sandwiches.

# Corn Soufflé

4 eggs
2 cups milk or half-and-half
3 15.25-ounce cans of corn, drained
½ teaspoon salt
2 tablespoons melted butter
2 tablespoons cornmeal
1 tablespoon flour
1 tablespoon granulated sugar

*

Preheat oven to 350°.

Mix eggs and milk together in a large mixing bowl. Add all remaining ingredients, stirring to combine. Pour into a 9 × 13-inch casserole or baking dish.

Bake for 45 minutes or until set.

*Serves 6 to 8.*

With one minute to go in a 1968 televised game between the New York Jets and the Oakland Raiders, the Jets led 32–29. Television executives made a decision to cut away to the children's special *Heidi* during a station break, but the Raiders rallied and scored two touchdowns in the final minute, winning the game 43–32. Unable to accommodate the volume of irate calls, the NBC switchboard blew a fuse. The *New York Daily News* headline the next day read "Raiders 43, Jets 32, Heidi 14."

On every team there are dependable players who never fail to deliver. Corn muffins are those players for football food. Easy to make, easily frozen, and quickly reheated or grilled, these are always a good choice and travel well to tailgates.

---

# Corn Muffins

1 cup all-purpose flour
1 cup yellow cornmeal
⅓ cup granulated sugar
2 teaspoons baking powder
1 teaspoon salt
½ teaspoon baking soda
1 cup sour cream
½ stick unsalted butter, melted and cooled
2 eggs
1 cup frozen corn kernels, thawed and drained

✳

Preheat the oven to 425°. Generously grease 12 muffin cups.

In a large bowl, combine the flour, cornmeal, sugar, baking powder, salt and baking soda.

In another medium bowl, whisk together the sour cream, melted butter, and eggs. Add the sour cream mixture to the dry ingredients and stir until just moistened. Fold in the corn kernels.

Divide the batter equally among the muffin cups. Bake about 20 minutes or until golden and a tester inserted in the center comes out clean.

Cool the muffins on a wire rack. Serve warm or at room temperature.

*Makes 12 muffins.*

This dish has never failed to please our guests and there are never any leftovers. You can assemble it early in the day, and then pop it in the oven just before the game.

# Onion-Cheddar Corn Bread

4 tablespoons unsalted butter
1 large onion, chopped
2 large eggs
2 tablespoons buttermilk
1 15-ounce can cream-style corn
1 1-pound package corn muffin mix
1 cup sour cream
2 cups grated sharp cheddar cheese

*

Preheat the oven to 425°. Generously grease an 8 × 11-inch baking dish.

In a medium skillet, heat the butter over medium-high heat and sauté the onions until golden brown, 10 to 15 minutes. Set aside to cool.

In a large bowl, combine the eggs and buttermilk and mix until smooth. Stir in the corn and the muffin mix. Spread the batter evenly into the prepared dish and spoon the onions over the top. Carefully spread the sour cream over the onions and top with the grated cheese.

Bake for about 30 minutes or until golden brown. Let stand 10 minutes before cutting. Serve warm or at room temperature.

*Serves 10 to 12.*

All-Pro Kansas City end Fred Arbanas was hit so hard in a 1965 game that his glass eye popped out. Referee Tommy Bell handed it to him and asked, "What would you do if the other eye was injured?" Arbanus replied, "I'd become a referee."

This garlic bread is a step up from the buttery broiled version we remember from our youth. Roasting the garlic brings out the sweetness and makes it creamy smooth. This is a great side dish for pasta or grilled meats.

## Roasted Garlic Bread

2 bulbs garlic
2–3 tablespoons olive oil
1 large loaf Italian bread
1 stick butter, softened
3 tablespoons grated Parmesan cheese

\*

Preheat the oven to 375°.

Slice the tops off the garlic bulbs so that the tip of each clove is exposed. Place the bulbs in the center of a piece of aluminum foil that is large enough to wrap around the bulbs. Drizzle the olive oil over the exposed cloves, seal the bulbs in the foil by making a little pouch, and bake for 35 to 40 minutes or until the garlic is very soft and fragrant.

In a medium bowl, combine the softened butter with the Parmesan. When the garlic is cool enough to touch, gently squeeze the cloves out of the bulb and into the bowl and mash together with a fork.

Slice the bread in half horizontally and spread the butter mixture evenly over the surface. Place the bread on a cookie sheet, cut side up, and run under the broiler for about 5 minutes or until lightly browned and bubbling. Slice thickly and serve.

*Serves 8 to 10.*

Simple, delicious, and universally loved, potato salad goes with just about any grilled dish or sandwiches. To save time, boil the potatoes the day before the game, cool, and keep refrigerated until you're ready to put the salad together.

# Potato Salad

1½ pounds russet potatoes, peeled and cubed
1 stalk celery, chopped
½ onion, chopped
2 hard-boiled eggs, chopped
1 tablespoon fresh flat leaf parsley, chopped
1–2 teaspoons mustard, optional
1 teaspoon seasoning salt
Freshly ground pepper to taste
1 cup mayonnaise or more if needed
Paprika

\*

Put the potatoes in a pot and cover with water. Bring to a boil and cook for about 10 minutes or until potatoes are easily pierced with a knife. Drain and cool.

In a large bowl, combine the potatoes, celery, onion, hard-boiled eggs, parsley, optional mustard, seasoning salt, and pepper.

Gently stir in the mayonnaise and combine. Cover and chill until ready to serve. Before serving, sprinkle paprika on the top of the salad for color.

*Serves 4 to 6.*

---

"When you played for Lombardi, anything other than death was a minor injury."

Bart Starr

A number of our friends admit to having "spud lust" in addition to their football addiction. This potato casserole is for those fans. It's easily made in advance and gently reheated. We serve it with grilled meats or meatloaf.

# Cheesy Potato Casserole

1 tablespoon butter
1 small onion, finely chopped, optional
3 large eggs
1½ cups whole milk
1 cup shredded Swiss cheese
½ teaspoon dry mustard
Pinch nutmeg
¾ teaspoon salt
½ teaspoon freshly ground pepper
4 large russet potatoes (about 2 pounds), peeled and shredded

\*

Preheat the oven to 375º. Grease a 9 × 13-inch baking dish.

In a medium skillet, melt the butter and sauté the onion until softened and translucent, about 5 minutes. Remove from the heat and cool.

In a large bowl, whisk together the eggs and milk. Stir in the onion, cheese, mustard, nutmeg, salt, and pepper. Add the shredded potatoes and toss to coat.

Pour into the prepared baking dish and bake for 55 to 60 minutes or until the potatoes are tender and the top of the casserole is starting to brown.

*Serves 4 to 6.*

\*

*Note*: To prevent the potatoes from turning brown, place them in cold water as you shred them. Drain the potatoes and squeeze them dry with paper towels when ready to use.

Sweet potatoes are plentiful in grocery stores during football season, and they roast beautifully. You can toss the ingredients together early in the day and just pop the dish in the oven during a commercial break. Serve with chicken or beef.

# Roasted Sweet Potatoes and Onions

2 large sweet potatoes (about 2 pounds), peeled and cut in 1" chunks
2 medium Vidalia or sweet onions, cut in 1" chunks
3 tablespoons olive oil
¼ cup Amaretto liqueur, optional
1 teaspoon dried thyme
Salt and freshly ground black pepper to taste
¼ cup sliced almonds, toasted

✳

Preheat oven to 425°.

In a large bowl, toss the sweet potatoes, onions, olive oil, optional Amaretto, thyme, salt, and pepper together. Spread in an ungreased 9 × 13-inch baking dish. Cover with aluminum foil and bake for 25 minutes.

Uncover the dish and bake an additional 20 minutes or until sweet potatoes and onions are easily pierced with a knife. Sprinkle the dish with the almonds and serve.

*Serves 6 to 8.*

"Some people think football is a matter of life and death. I don't like that attitude. I can assure them it is much more serious than that."

Bill Shankly

The big advantage to this dish is that you can use any vegetable combination you like. The trick is to make sure all the vegetables are cut into chunks of about the same size so that they cook evenly. Make a big batch on Sunday and enjoy them all week.

# Roasted Fall Vegetables

6 cups assorted fall vegetables, peeled and cut in 1 ½"
    chunks (use sweet potatoes, carrots, turnips, parsnips,
    butternut squash, etc.)
6 tablespoons extra-virgin olive oil
1 tablespoon fresh thyme leaves
Salt and pepper to taste

*

Preheat oven to 400°.

In a large bowl, toss the vegetables with olive oil, thyme, salt, and pepper. Spread the vegetables on a baking sheet, in a single layer.

Roast for 45 to 55 minutes, stirring occasionally, until the vegetables are tender and beginning to brown. Adjust the seasonings and serve.

*Serves 6 to 8.*

> "Football is, after all, a wonderful way to get rid of your aggressions without going to jail for it."
>
> Heywood Hale Brown

They say necessity is the mother of invention, and in this case it's true. With a crowd of 28 for the Super Bowl and no extra plates on hand, the only way to serve the salad was to wrap it in a tortilla! These are great with grilled meats and poultry.

# Mexican Salad Burritos

2½ cups chopped romaine lettuce
1 15½-ounce can black beans, well drained
¾ cup seeded tomato, chopped
¾ cup corn kernels, fresh, frozen or canned
Half a ripe avocado, diced
1 red bell pepper, chopped
¼ cup feta cheese, crumbled

## Honey-Lime Dressing

¼ cup fresh lime juice
¼ cup olive oil
2 tablespoons honey
2 tablespoons fresh cilantro, chopped (or more to taste)
1 garlic clove, minced
1 teaspoon jalapeño pepper, minced

*

Flour tortillas

*

In a large serving bowl, toss the salad ingredients. In a medium bowl, whisk together the dressing ingredients. Season to taste with salt and pepper. Pour dressing over mixture and toss again.

Place 1 cup salad in the lower third of a flour tortilla and wrap tightly as though making a burrito. Cut each tortilla in half and arrange halves on a brightly colored platter.

*Serves 6 to 8.*

One of Maili's earliest creations, this hearty salad is easily transported to tailgates or a friend's house for a televised game. It can be served for lunch or dinner. Serve with mojitos or beer.

## Curried Chicken Pasta Salad

1 pound tri-colored rotini pasta
4 boneless skinless chicken breasts
1 tablespoon oil or nonstick cooking spray
1 teaspoon salt
2 teaspoons curry powder
½ cup raisins
2 11-ounce cans mandarin oranges, drained
¼ cup mayonnaise
½ cup roasted almonds, chopped or sliced

*

Cook pasta in boiling salted water according to package instructions. Rinse with cold water until completely cool; drain, place in a large mixing bowl, and set aside.

Cut chicken into bite-sized pieces. Heat a large nonstick frying pan on medium-high heat. Spray with nonstick cooking spray or oil, then add chicken and season with ½ teaspoon salt and 1 teaspoon curry powder. Stir with a spoon until chicken is cooked through, about 6 to 8 minutes.

Remove the chicken from heat and add to pasta. Add the raisins, mandarin oranges, mayonnaise, roasted almonds, remaining 1 teaspoon curry powder and ½ teaspoon salt. Combine well and serve.

The pasta salad can be made a day or two in advance and kept refrigerated.

*Serves 6 to 8.*

We love any side dish that can be made ahead and doesn't require last minute attention, so this recipe contributed by a die-hard Patriots fan makes our list of favorites. It goes well with grilled meats or Auntie Fran's Baby Back Ribs.

---

## Macaroni Salad

1 12-ounce box penne pasta

1 jar sun-dried tomatoes, marinated in olive oil

1 2.25-ounce can sliced black olives

1 small green pepper, diced

1 cup fresh broccoli florets, cut in bite-sized pieces, optional

½ teaspoon garlic and herb seasoning of your choice

1 teaspoon parsley, chopped

Salt and pepper to taste

1 cup mayonnaise

¼ cup ketchup

\*

Cook pasta according to package instructions. Drain and set aside in a serving bowl.

Strain the sun-dried tomatoes and pat lightly with paper towels to remove excess olive oil. Add the tomatoes, olives, diced peppers, and broccoli to the pasta. Add the seasoning, parsley, and salt and pepper to taste.

In a separate bowl, combine the mayonnaise and ketchup until blended. Stir into the pasta and vegetables and chill at least one hour before serving.

*Serves 6 to 8.*

> "We can't run. We can't pass. We can't stop the run. We can't stop the pass. We can't kick. Other than that, we're just not a very good football team right now."
>
> Bruce Coslet, on the Bengals' 1997 season

The secret to this delicious salad is the mint. It's amazing how such a small ingredient makes such a huge difference. The salad can be made long before kick-off or a tailgate event, then just toss in the pecans at the last minute so that they stay crisp.

# Gridiron Green Bean Salad

1 teaspoon salt

1½ pounds fresh green beans, stem ends trimmed

4 ounces feta cheese, crumbled

1 cup pecans, roasted

1–2 tablespoons mint, finely chopped

⅓ cup your favorite balsamic dressing (or use ours below)

## Balsamic Vinaigrette

1 teaspoon coarse ground mustard

½ teaspoon kosher salt

¼ teaspoon freshly ground pepper

½ cup balsamic vinegar

1¼ cup olive oil

2 tablespoons water

1 tablespoon granulated sugar

\*

Add the salt to a 6- to 8-quart saucepan of water and bring to a boil. Once the water boils, add the green beans and blanch for 3 minutes. You want them to have a little crunch to them. Immediately rinse the beans in cold water until cooled. Drain.

In a bowl, toss the green beans, feta cheese, pecans, mint, and ⅓ cup of the balsamic dressing. Combine well.

To make the dressing, place all ingredients except the oil in a blender and blend briefly to combine. With the motor running on low, very gradually add the olive oil in a steady stream through the hole in the top of the blender lid until the dressing is emulsified. The remaining dressing will keep in the refrigerator for months and can be used on any green salad.

*Serves 6 to 8.*

\*

*Note*: To roast pecans, place in a 375° oven for 8 to 10 minutes. Stay close so they don't burn.

*Note*: The easiest way to chop mint is to roll all the leaves together and then make thin slices.

Leta B was a staunch Nebraska Cornhusker fan, a great home cook, and Kellie's grandmother. This is her recipe for coleslaw to feed a crowd during championship games against the archrival Oklahoma Sooners.

---

## Leta B's Coleslaw

3 cups shredded cabbage (green or a combination of green and red)
½–⅔ cup shredded carrots
1 scant tablespoon lemon juice
⅓ cup + 1 tablespoon Hellman's mayonnaise
½ teaspoon granulated sugar
Paprika, optional

*

In a large bowl, mix all the ingredients and adjust the seasonings. Dust the top with paprika for color if desired.

*Serves 6 to 8.*

# End Zone Celebrations

## Our Best Sweet Conclusions

Seasoned football fans live for games that are decided in the last seconds of the fourth quarter. It doesn't happen often, but when it does, it's a thing of beauty. With these cliffhanger endings you're never quite sure—is it divine intervention or pure luck?

During the 1975 playoffs Cowboys quarterback Roger Staubach coined a new phrase when he connected with Drew Pearson for an astonishing, game-winning, 50-yard reception. With less than a minute on the clock, Staubach launched a desperate bomb he later referred to as a "Hail Mary" pass. "You just throw it up and hope your man comes down with it," Boston College coach Jack Bicknell later said. "Of course, you don't expect it to happen."

In California it's simply called The Big Game. In 1982 John Elway, in his last season as a Stanford Cardinal, found himself at 4th and 17 on his own 13-yard line with 53 seconds remaining. Elway completed a pass for a 29-yard gain, and with 4 seconds left, Mark Harmon kicked a 35-yard field goal to put Stanford up 20–19. Game over? Not quite. Berkeley still had a final play, and what happened next is nothing less than college football legend.

Berkeley received the kick-off on their own 43-yard line and executed five lateral passes before Kevin Moen sprinted into the end zone. Of course he had to artfully dodge the Stanford marching band to get there. Believing victory was in hand, the exuberant musicians—trombones included—rushed the field, making it all but impossible for the Cardinals to catch Moen. The game ended in complete pandemonium—Berkeley 25, Stanford 20.

Then there was the 1972 playoff game between the Oakland Raiders and the Pittsburgh Steelers. With 22 seconds left in the fourth quarter, the Raiders led the Steelers 7–6. At 4th and 10, Steelers quarterback Terry Bradshaw scrambled out of the pocket to throw a long bomb deep into Raiders territory. The ball bounced off a defender's chest and into the hands of Steelers' blocker Franco Harris. Under NFL rules Harris was ineligible to receive the ball—unless a defensive player had already touched it. Harris ran in for a touchdown and the Steelers won the game 13–7. To this day it is referred to as The Immaculate Reception.

These and other great endings are what make being a fan so much fun. The last place you want to be when history is made is in the kitchen fussing with your own great ending— dessert. This chapter features sweet treats made well in advance for you to set out during a commercial break late in the game. Cookies, brownies, and dessert bars are easily eaten with fingers, don't require additional plates, and are always welcomed by fans who refuse to move from the couch. We put the coffee on during the third quarter so as to be glued to the television—not the stove—as the last minutes on the game clock tick down.

Dessert bars are our favorite way to satisfy our fans' sweet tooth because they can be made a day in advance and make their grand appearance during a commercial break late in the game—no last minute fussing necessary. This dessert offers a sweet surprise in the raspberry layer hiding beneath the surface.

# Raspberry Oatmeal Bars

1½ cups sifted flour
1 teaspoon baking powder
¼ teaspoon salt
1 cup dark brown sugar
2 sticks cold, unsalted butter, cut into cubes
1¼ cups quick cooking oats
1 12-ounce jar raspberry preserves

✳

Preheat the oven to 375°. Butter a 9 × 13-inch baking dish.

In a food processor, combine the flour, baking powder, salt, and brown sugar. Add the butter and pulse 10 to 12 times until the mixture resembles coarse meal. Pour the mixture into a large bowl and stir in the oats.

Place ⅔ of the mixture in the prepared baking dish. Carefully spread the preserves in a smooth layer on top. Cover with the remaining crumb mixture.

Bake for 35 minutes or until golden brown. Remove from oven and cool completely before cutting into squares.

*Makes 24 squares.*

> "Setting a goal is not the main thing. It is deciding how you will go about achieving it and staying with that plan."
>
> Tom Landry

This recipe hails from Kellie's grandmother, Margaret, who married a die-hard USC fan and quickly became one herself. We like the dish with sliced almonds, but chopped hazelnuts work just as well.

# Almond Taffy Bars

1 stick unsalted butter, softened
1½ cups lightly packed brown sugar
1 cup sifted flour
2 eggs
1 teaspoon vanilla
2 tablespoons flour
1 teaspoon baking powder
½ teaspoon salt
1 cup shredded coconut
1 cup sliced almonds (or substitute roasted,
   chopped hazelnuts)

\*

Preheat the oven to 350°. Butter an 8 × 11-inch baking dish.

In an electric mixer, cream the butter and ½ cup of the brown sugar. Add 1 cup flour and beat until combined. Gently press the batter into the prepared baking dish and bake for 10 minutes.

Meanwhile, beat the eggs, add the remaining 1 cup brown sugar and vanilla and combine. Add the flour, baking powder, and salt and stir. Add the coconut and almonds and stir until combined.

Spread the topping gently over the bottom layer and return to the oven. Bake for 25 minutes or until topping is golden brown.

*Makes 24 squares.*

These brownies are incredibly decadent and not for the faint of heart! When it's late in the fourth quarter and it looks as though we may actually pull off a conference championship spot, we like to reach for these rich, creamy treats to celebrate.

# Excessive Celebration Peanut Butter Brownies

1 stick unsalted butter
½ cup peanut butter
1½ cups granulated sugar
3 eggs
1 cup flour
½ teaspoon salt
1 teaspoon vanilla
6 ounces semisweet chocolate chips
1 cup pecans, chopped

## Topping

1 cup peanut butter
½ cup powdered sugar
1 teaspoon vanilla
½ stick unsalted butter
6 ounces semisweet chocolate chips

*

Preheat the oven to 350º. Butter a 9 × 13-inch pan.

Cream the butter and peanut butter in an electric mixer. Gradually add the sugar at medium speed. Beat until smooth and creamy. Add the eggs, one at a time, mixing thoroughly after each addition.

Stir in the flour and salt. When combined, add the vanilla. Stir in the chocolate chips and pecans.

Spread the batter into the baking dish. Bake for 30 minutes or until lightly browned. Cool completely before adding the topping.

To make the topping, cream the peanut butter, powdered sugar, and vanilla in an electric mixer. Spread the mixture evenly over the brownies.

In a small saucepan over very low heat, melt the butter, add the chocolate chips, and stir constantly until the chocolate is melted. Pour the chocolate mixture over the peanut butter frosting layer, smoothing it out in an even layer. Refrigerate the brownies until the topping hardens.

Cool and cut into squares.

*Makes 24 brownies.*

---

"If you don't make a total commitment to whatever you're doing, then you start looking to bail out the first time the boat starts leaking. It's tough enough getting that boat to shore with everybody rowing, let alone when a guy stands up and starts putting his jacket on."

Notre Dame coach Lou Holtz

Kellie found this recipe on a wine-tasting tour through Sonoma several years ago, and it quickly became a fourth quarter favorite. Once they cool, cut the brownies into squares; they keep in an airtight container for up to three days.

# Merlot Brownies

4 ounces bittersweet chocolate

1 ½ sticks unsalted butter

1 cup Merlot wine, reduced to ¼ cup

3 eggs

2 cups granulated sugar

1 teaspoon vanilla

1 cup flour

1 cup coarsely chopped pecans

*

Preheat the oven to 350°. Grease a 9 × 13-inch pan.

Melt the chocolate and butter together in a double boiler. Remove from the heat and add the reduced wine.

Combine the eggs, sugar, and vanilla in a double boiler and heat to 110°, transfer to an electric mixer, and whip until medium peaks form.

In a large bowl, combine the chocolate and wine mixture with the egg batter. Fold in the flour and ½ cup of the pecans.

Spread the batter into the prepared pan and sprinkle the remaining pecans on top. Bake for 45 minutes or until a toothpick comes out clean.

*Makes 12 brownies.*

*

*Note*: To reduce the wine, pour it into a heavy saucepan and bring to a boil. Reduce the heat and simmer uncovered for 30 to 40 minutes or until reduced to ¼ cup.

A tried and true favorite, these cookies have been served to fans from California to New Hampshire. Make them up to three days in advance and keep in an airtight container.

# Cinnamon Chocolate Chip Cookies

¾ cup brown sugar

¾ cup granulated sugar

1 cup Crisco shortening

2 eggs, beaten

1 teaspoon ground cinnamon

1 teaspoon vanilla

1 teaspoon warm water added to 1 teaspoon baking soda

2¼ cups flour

1 teaspoon salt

1 6-ounce package chocolate chips

1 cup chopped walnuts

✳

Preheat oven to 350°. Grease a cookie sheet.

In a large bowl, cream together the sugars and shortening. Add the eggs, cinnamon, vanilla, and the water and baking soda mixture.

Sift together the flour and salt and add to the cookie dough. Stir in the chocolate chips and nuts.

Drop the dough onto the prepared cookie sheet by spoonfuls. Bake for 12 to 14 minutes or until cookies are just beginning to brown. Cool on a rack.

*Makes about 3 dozen cookies.*

> "Gentlemen, it is better to have died as a small boy than to fumble this football."
>
> John Heisman

Just as the name implies, these cookies have it all, and they never fail to receive rave reviews. For big games, we use an ice cream scoop to make giant cookies that wow the crowd.

# Everything-but-the-Kitchen-Sink Cookies

2 sticks unsalted butter, softened
1 cup granulated sugar
1 cup brown sugar, packed
1 egg, lightly beaten
1 cup vegetable oil
2 teaspoons vanilla
1 cup cornflakes, crushed
3½ cups sifted flour
1 teaspoon baking soda
½ teaspoon salt
1 cup rolled oats
½ cup flaked coconut
½ cup pecans, chopped
½ cup macadamia nuts, chopped
½ cup chocolate chips
½ cup raisins

\*

Preheat the oven to 325º.

In an electric mixer, cream the butter and sugars together until light and fluffy. Stir in the egg, oil, and vanilla. Add the cornflakes and mix until well combined.

Sift the flour with the baking soda and salt into the butter-sugar mixture. Stir to combine, then add the oats, coconut, pecans, macadamia nuts, chocolate chips, and raisins. Stir until all the ingredients are well mixed.

Using a large tablespoon of dough for each cookie, place spoonfuls on an ungreased cookie sheet, about 2 inches apart. Flatten the tops slightly with a fork.

Bake for 10 to 12 minutes or until lightly brown. Remove the cookies from the baking sheet, let stand for several minutes, and then transfer to a wire rack to cool completely.

*Makes about 4 dozen cookies.*

> **"It's not the size of the dog in the fight, but the size of the fight in the dog."**
>
> Archie Griffen, two-time Heisman winner

Maili has been serving these cookies at football parties for years. They're kid-tested and approved, and they travel well to tailgates.

# Chocolate Chip Crunch Cookies

2 cups all-purpose flour
½ cup old-fashioned oats
1 teaspoon baking soda
1 teaspoon salt
2 sticks (1 cup) unsalted butter, softened
1 cup light brown sugar
½ cup granulated sugar
2 eggs
1 teaspoon pure vanilla extract
2 cups chocolate chips
1½ cups crispy rice cereal
½ cup raisins, optional

\*

Preheat oven to 375°.

In a small bowl, combine the flour, oats, baking soda, and salt.

In the large bowl of an electric mixer, or with a bowl and hand-held mixer, cream the butter, brown sugar, and granulated sugar. Add the eggs one at a time, beating until combined.

Add the dry ingredients a half cup at a time, beating shortly after each addition until dry mixture is incorporated.

Add the vanilla and combine. Add the chocolate chips, crispy rice cereal, and the optional raisins. Stir briefly until just combined.

Place heaping tablespoons of dough at least 2 inches apart on an ungreased baking sheet. Bake cookies in the middle of the oven for 9 to 12 minutes, or until they are just golden.

Remove from oven and cool on pans for 2 minutes. Transfer with a thin metal spatula to a wire rack to finish cooling. Store in an airtight container.

*Makes about 3 dozen cookies.*

When Maili decided she needed the ultimate peanut butter cookie for a playoff party, she tested over 300 cookies to perfect the recipe. After a blind taste testing, this version won unanimously.

---

# Point After Peanut Butter Cookies

1½ sticks unsalted butter, softened
1 ½ cups peanut butter
1 cup dark brown sugar
½ cup granulated sugar, plus enough to coat dough balls
2 eggs
2 teaspoons vanilla
1¼ cup unbleached flour
1 teaspoon baking soda
¼ teaspoon salt

&ast;

Preheat oven to 350°.

In a mixer, cream the butter, peanut butter, and sugars together until well blended. Add eggs and vanilla and stir to combine.

In a separate bowl, combine the flour, baking soda, and salt. Add dry ingredients to the peanut butter mixture. The dough will be *very* sticky.

Place extra sugar in a shallow plate for rolling the dough. Roll dough in the palm of your hands into 1½" balls and roll the balls in the sugar. Place on parchment-lined baking sheet pans or ungreased cookie sheet pans. Press with fork tines to make a criss-cross pattern on the cookie.

Bake 14 to 16 minutes, but do not overbake or the cookies will be dry. Cool on cookie sheets for 2 minutes and then transfer to a wire rack to cool.

*Makes 3 to 4 dozen cookies.*

These oatmeal cookies have attitude! The butterscotch chips make them sweet, but the black walnuts give them texture and deep, rich flavor. Easily made the day before the game, they can be transported to tailgate parties in an airtight container.

# Black Walnut and Butterscotch Cookies

2 sticks unsalted butter
1 cup granulated sugar
1 cup brown sugar
2 eggs
2 cups flour
1 teaspoon baking soda
½ teaspoon salt
½ teaspoon baking powder
1 cup rolled oats
6 ounces butterscotch chips
½ cup black walnuts, chopped

\*

Preheat oven to 350º.

Cream the butter and sugars until light and fluffy. Add the eggs one at a time, beating well after each addition.

Sift the flour, baking soda, salt, and baking powder together and mix into the egg mixture. If using an electric mixer, remove the bowl and use a spoon to add the oats, butterscotch chips, and walnuts.

Drop by large tablespoonfuls onto a greased cookie sheet. Bake for 12 to 14 minutes or until edges start to brown. Let the cookies cool on the cookie sheet for 2 minutes before transferring to a cooling rack.

*Makes about 3 dozen cookies.*

Whether to add nuts and/or raisins to pumpkin bread is as hotly debated as the question of artificial turf vs. grass. Go with whatever gets you the most compliments! This is a great tailgate dessert because it can be made in advance and travels so well.

## Pumpkin Bread

3½ cups unbleached flour
2 teaspoons baking powder
2 teaspoons baking soda
1½ teaspoons salt
2 teaspoons ground cinnamon
1 teaspoon nutmeg
1 teaspoon ground cloves
2 teaspoons ground ginger
2 teaspoons crystallized ginger, minced, optional
2 sticks unsalted butter, softened (or vegetable oil)
1 cup granulated sugar
1½ cups dark brown sugar
3 cups pure canned pumpkin
4 eggs
½ cup sour cream
½ cup raisins, optional
1 cup roasted walnuts or pecans, optional

\*

Preheat oven to 375°. Grease 2 loaf pans with butter or non-stick cooking spray.

Mix the flour, baking powder, baking soda, salt, cinnamon, nutmeg, cloves, ginger, and crystallized ginger thoroughly in a large bowl.

Cream the butter (or oil) and both sugars in an electric mixer. Add the pumpkin and mix again. Add the eggs one by one, beating after each addition.

Add the sour cream and then the flour mixture, one cup at a time. After each addition, incorporate the flour thoroughly. Add raisins and nuts if desired.

Divide batter evenly between the two loaf pans. Bake for 1 hour, or until a toothpick inserted in the center comes out clean. Cool in pans 5 minutes, then remove bread from pans to cool completely on cooling racks.

*Makes two loaves.*

> "Pro football gave me a good sense of perspective to enter politics. I've been booed, cheered, cut, sold, traded and hung in effigy."
>
> Jack Kemp

The secret to this dish is not telling anyone there's zucchini in it. It's moist, chocolaty, and made in advance, and it unobtrusively delivers vegetables to unsuspecting children.

---

# Chocolate Zucchini Cake

1 cup brown sugar
½ cup granulated sugar
1 stick unsalted butter
½ cup vegetable oil
3 eggs
1 teaspoon vanilla
½ cup buttermilk
2½ cups flour
½ teaspoon allspice
½ teaspoon ground cinnamon
½ teaspoon salt
2 teaspoons baking soda
4 tablespoons cocoa
2½ cups grated zucchini
1 cup chocolate chips

\*

Preheat the oven to 325°. Grease and flour a 9 × 13-inch baking pan.

In an electric mixer, cream the sugars, butter, and oil until light and fluffy. Add the eggs, vanilla, and buttermilk and beat well.

Sift the flour, allspice, cinnamon, salt, baking soda, and cocoa together and mix into the batter. Add the grated zucchini and stir until combined.

Pour into the prepared pan and sprinkle the chocolate chips on top.

Bake for 55 to 65 minutes or until a toothpick inserted in the middle comes out clean.

*Serves 8 to 10.*

Apple Pandowdy is a dessert that's been around as long as football. It's also a nice finish to a relaxed afternoon game. While it does require some game day maintenance, this can be done during commercial breaks and it's worth it.

# Apple Pandowdy

3 cups apples, peeled, cored, and thinly sliced
⅓ cup packed dark brown sugar
¼ teaspoon ground cinnamon
¼ teaspoon nutmeg
½ stick unsalted butter
½ cup granulated sugar
1 egg
¾ cup flour
¾ teaspoon baking powder
¼ teaspoon salt
⅓ cup milk
¾ cup cream

\*

Preheat oven to 375°. Butter a 1-quart baking dish.

In a large bowl, toss the apples with the brown sugar, cinnamon, and nutmeg. Pour into the prepared dish and bake for 30 minutes.

Meanwhile, cream the butter and gradually add the sugar and beat until fluffy. Add the egg and beat well. Sift the dry ingredients and add to the batter alternately with the milk. Beat until smooth.

Spread the batter evenly over the cooked apples; return to the oven and bake for an additional 30 minutes. Serve the Pandowdy warm with cream poured over the top.

*Serves 4 to 6.*

Nothing says football season and fall like apple pie. Our version includes all the spices reminiscent of the season and has flavor to spare. Bake it the morning of the game and simply slice and serve during the fourth quarter.

---

# Caramel Apple Pie

2 piecrusts for 9-inch pie
6–8 Granny Smith apples, peeled, cored, and sliced
1 tablespoon lemon juice
¼ cup granulated sugar
¾ cup packed dark brown sugar
Pinch of salt
⅓ cup flour
¼ teaspoon nutmeg
⅛ teaspoon ground cloves
½ teaspoon ground cinnamon
2 tablespoons butter, diced
1 egg white
2 tablespoons granulated sugar combined with ¼ teaspoon
  ground cinnamon

*

Preheat the oven to 375°. Line a 9-inch pie plate with pastry.

In a large bowl, sprinkle the sliced apples with the lemon juice. In a small bowl, mix together the sugars, salt, flour, nutmeg, cloves, and cinnamon; add to the apples and toss to coat.

Gently pour the apple mixture into the pastry-lined pie plate. Dot with the butter and top with the second piecrust. Seal the piecrusts by crimping the edges together with your fingers or fork tines. Using a paring knife, cut four small steam vents in the top crust.

In a small bowl, whisk the egg white until foamy. Brush the top of the pie with the egg white and sprinkle with the cinnamon sugar.

Place the pie on a cookie sheet and bake for 45 to 50 minutes or until the apples are easily pierced with a knife. Allow the pie to cool on a rack for 15 minutes before serving.

*Serves 6 to 8.*

During a preseason game against Pittsburgh, Bears coach George Halas called then-rookie Lionel Taylor off the bench and explained, "We're out of timeouts. Go out there and get hurt." Taylor would go on to become a five-time leading AFL receiver with the Denver Broncos.

This toffee is so dangerously good that we can eat the entire batch by ourselves. You can keep it simple by putting chocolate and almonds on only one side, or go the extra step and coat both sides. It can be made up to a month in advance and travels in an airtight container, so this is a great tailgate option.

## Tailgate Toffee

¾ cup roasted almonds, coarsely chopped
¾ cup finely ground almonds
2 sticks unsalted butter
1⅓ cups granulated sugar
1 tablespoon corn syrup
1 tablespoon water
1 tablespoon vanilla
1 cup semisweet chocolate chips
1 cup semisweet chocolate chips, for second side

✳

Generously butter a 9 × 13-inch metal baking sheet with at least ¾" sides. You must use butter for this, not nonstick cooking spray.

In a 3-quart saucepan, melt the butter over low heat. Add the sugar, corn syrup, water, and vanilla. Stir with a wooden spoon until the sugar dissolves.

Once the sugar has dissolved, clip a candy thermometer to the side of the pan, making sure it doesn't rest against the bottom of the pan. Increase the heat to high and allow the mixture to come to a roiling boil. Don't stir the toffee mixture as it boils. It will take between 5 and 7 minutes to reach 290°. Watch closely as the temperature rises, as it will accelerate quickly when it gets close to 290°.

When it reaches 290°, stir in the chopped almonds. Do not scrape the sides. The whole mixture will lump and come out in a ball. Smooth the mixture into the buttered pan with the back of a spoon.

Allow to cool for 2 minutes, then sprinkle one cup chocolate chips over the hot toffee. The heat from the toffee will melt the chocolate. Use an off-set spatula or the back of the spoon and spread the chocolate in a smooth layer over the toffee. Sprinkle the finely ground almonds on top of the chocolate. Let cool until chocolate is hard.

You can stop here if you want chocolate on only one side. If you want chocolate on both sides, cover the cooled toffee with wax paper, invert the pan, and bang on the back until the toffee pops out.

Melt the additional cup of chocolate chips in the microwave. Spread on the back of the toffee and sprinkle with nuts.

Once it's cool, break the toffee into shards. It can be made a month in advance and kept in an airtight container in a cool, dry place.

*Serves 4.*

> When Rams defensive end Jack Youngblood broke his leg in a 1979 playoff game, he asked the doctors to tape it up. When the doctors explained that you can't tape a broken fibula, Youngblood refused to be deterred and replied, "Tape two aspirin to it."

# Surviving the Off-Season

It happens every year—Black Sunday arrives. The Pro Bowl is played the second Saturday in February, and the following day reality sets in for millions of fans worldwide. It's the off-season. No more *Monday Night Football*, no more Saturday afternoon college games, and Sunday nights spent screaming at the television are a thing of the past. It will be five long months until the first NFL exhibition game is played in July.

If you're a basketball fan, you simply switch gears, settle down, and watch men in shorts run back and forth across the court for a measly two points per basket. If you're a baseball fan, you can call the cable company, sign up for an extended package, and follow spring training.

But if you're a die-hard football fan, it's a time of darkness and despair. Sundays are just another day, and Monday nights are long evenings filled with sitcoms and crime scene investigations unfolding. Here are some ways we've found to help combat the withdrawal.

### Arena Football

Debuting with its first game in 1986, the Arena Football League consists of 19 teams that play from the first week of March until late July. Playing indoors on a 50-yard field, the American Conference League and the National Conference League battle it out with eight men on the field for each team and a 20-man active roster. The season finale—the Arena Bowl—is played just a few short weeks before the first NFL exhibition games.

ESPN and the AFL have recently signed a contract that makes it easier to catch the games on cable. Contact your cable provider to find out what your access might be. You can learn more about Arena Football at www.arenafootball.com.

## Substitutes

When cold Sunday afternoons drag out and the first exhibition game isn't even in sight, we prepare our favorite finger foods and pop in one of these football movies at 1:00 p.m. (kick-off time during the regular season):

*The Replacements*
*Any Given Sunday*
*Friday Night Lights*
*Remember the Titans*
*The Longest Yard*
*Necessary Roughness*
*Program*
*Wildcats*
*Monday Night Mayhem*

## The Glory Days

Every team has at least one video of their best year, and if you're lucky your team has had a string of successful seasons with the highlights captured on DVD or video. Check out your team's Web site and see if you can find a copy or, at the very least, a team history. This has kept us going when the off-season gets rough.

Highlights and great moments from every Super Bowl are available on DVD through most movie rental outlets or on-line at www.nfl.com. During the football drought, we invite friends over, set out a party spread, and watch a favorite Super Bowl game. The advantage of the DVD is that you can view the player highlights and extras as a sort of pregame event. You don't get the commercials, but it's almost like the first Sunday in February!

## Follow the Draft

On the third weekend in April, there is a glimmer of light at the end of the dark tunnel—NFL Draft weekend. This televised event lets you see which college players will be your team's rookies during the approaching season. We've been known to invite over some friends who root for less talented teams, hand everyone a referee flag, and let them go at it when draft picks are announced. Reality will set in soon enough, so sit back in April, enjoy some football food, and imagine that each of these rookies will actually become an All-Pro player and make it through the season without injury. Go ahead and dream!

# Beyond Beer

## Sure-Fire Thirst Quenchers

While it's true that beer is the beverage of choice at college athletic events, it was advertising executives who carefully nurtured our perception of beer as the "official" beverage of football, starting in the early 1970s. Tobacco behemoth Philip Morris acquired Miller Brewing Company in 1970 and quickly made plans to replicate its Marlboro Man campaign success in the beer industry. Redrafting the rugged "man's man" image that increased cigarette sales by 5,000 percent, Philip Morris launched a series of television commercials featuring the toughest guys they could find—Matt Snell, John Madden, Dick Butkus, and Bubba Smith.

By the mid-70s, football was the most popular sport in America. A young quarterback named Joe Namath helped catapult the game into pop culture, *Monday Night Football* enjoyed the highest ratings in prime time, and American breweries were along for the joyride. The campaign slogans "For all you do, this Bud's for you," "If you've got the time, we've got the beer," and "Everything you always wanted in a beer—and less" were about the beer drinker, not the game—but they were now intrinsically linked in the minds of millions of television viewers. "Sissy" drinks were reserved for other occasions.

Today football fans come from every walk of life—male, female, young, old, young at heart, old in spirit, city dwellers, and suburbanites—and while beer is still a staple, we like to offer a variety of beverages at our get-togethers. Beyond Beer is a collection of cocktails that complements football fare and offers our guests some delicious options.

The "Hail Mary" pass was coined by Dallas quarterback Roger Staubach during a 1979 playoff game. Staubach launched a desperate bomb deep into enemy territory with less than a minute on the clock—connecting with Drew Pearson for a 50-yard reception and a Dallas win. Our spicy version of this classic drink celebrates that great moment.

## Bloody Hail Mary

1 cup vodka
3 cups tomato juice
½ teaspoon Tabasco sauce
1 teaspoon Worcestershire sauce
½ teaspoon freshly ground pepper
2 teaspoons prepared horseradish
½ teaspoon celery salt, optional
4 celery stalks with leaves

\*

Combine the first 7 ingredients in a blender or large cocktail shaker and mix. Pour into 4 large highball glasses filled with ice. Garnish with celery stalks.

*Serves 4.*

This cocktail is a variation on the Bloody Mary. Rumor has it that a bartender in the famous Savoy Hotel mixed it up for a Sunday morning guest who didn't like tomato juice. It makes a nice complement to brunch fare.

## Bull Shot

1½ ounces vodka
3 ounces beef bouillon, chilled
1 dash Worcestershire sauce
1 dash salt
1 dash black pepper

\*

Combine the ingredients in a cocktail shaker with ice and shake. Strain into an old-fashioned glass and serve.

*Serves 1.*

The first known professional player was William "Pudge" Heffelfinger, who was paid $500 under the table by a club in Pittsburgh in 1892.

The Mojito is a Cuban cousin of the Mint Julep. It's light and refreshing on warm nights early in the season. Enjoy this cocktail with grilled meats.

# Mojito

1 tablespoon fresh mint leaves
2 teaspoons granulated sugar
3 tablespoons fresh lemon juice
2 ounces light rum
Chilled club soda

\*

In a tall thin glass, crush the mint and sugar together using the handle of a wooden spoon. You want to smash up the mint leaves to release their oils and flavor. Add the lemon juice and rum and stir. Fill the glass with ice and then top off with the chilled club soda. Garnish with a fresh mint sprig.

*Serves 1.*

All but forgotten by modern mixologists, this drink was once called the "fried-egg sandwich of American mixology" by master hooch-ologist David Wondrich. We love whiskey sours because they're easy to make and go so well with football food. Blend them up on Sunday evening before kick-off.

# Whiskey Sours over Ice

6 ounces whiskey
20 ounces sour mix
3 tablespoons cherry juice or grenadine
8 squirts Angostura bitters
Orange slices
Maraschino cherries

＊

In a blender or large cocktail shaker, mix the whiskey, sour mix, cherry juice, and bitters. Fill 4 small cocktail glasses with ice. Pour the whiskey sours over the ice and garnish with orange slices and/or cherries.

*Serves 4.*

---

**"My knees look like they lost a knife fight with a midget."**

E. J. Holub, former Kansas City Chiefs linebacker, on his 12 knee surgeries.

This is an interesting twist on an old favorite. The color is gorgeous, and the drink is a great choice with grilled food. You can find peeled mango in jars in the produce section at the grocery store.

# Mango Margaritas

4 ounces Tequila
1 ounce Triple Sec liqueur
1 cup mango, fresh, jarred, or canned
2 cups ice

\*

In a blender, combine the Tequila, Triple Sec, mango, and ice. Blend until smooth. This recipe doubles easily.

*Serves 2.*

> "When I went to Catholic high school in Philadelphia, we just had one coach for football and basketball. He took all of us who turned out and had us run through a forest. The ones who ran into the trees were on the football team."
>
> George Raveling

There are as many stories depicting this cocktail's history as there are recipes for it. Our favorite—and the most romantic—is that Enrique Gutierrez created this drink in the 1940s for Rita Hayworth, whose real name was Margarita. The classic recipe calls for Tequila, Triple Sec or Cointreau, and fresh lime juice. We don't find this practical for large crowds, so we've substituted limeade. Sorry, Enrique!

# Margaritas

1 12-ounce can frozen limeade
12 ounces Tequila
6 ounces Triple Sec or Cointreau liqueur

✳

Empty the limeade into a blender. Fill the limeade can with Tequila and add to blender. Put in ½ can Triple Sec or Cointreau. Blend until smooth. Pour the margaritas over ice, garnish with slices of lime, and serve. You can easily double this recipe and have the margaritas waiting in a pitcher in the refrigerator.

*Serves 8, or 16 when doubled.*

This is a great choice for an early season game when you're running short on time. It can stay in the freezer for weeks; simply let it warm up to slush consistency while you're putting the finishing touches on your meal.

---

## Bourbon Slush

3½ cups water
6 ounces frozen lemonade
3 ounces frozen orange juice concentrate
1 cup strong black tea
¾ cup granulated sugar
1½ cups bourbon

✳

Combine all the ingredients in a freezer-safe container at least one day prior to serving and freeze. Before serving, remove from the freezer and allow the mixture to come to a slushy consistency, 10 to 20 minutes. Serve over ice.

*Makes 8 cups.*

This is a favorite on the West Coast, where the weather stays warm all the way to the Pro Bowl. It can be made days in advance and stored in the freezer, so it's the perfect last minute cocktail.

# Red Dunebuggy

16 ounces cranberry juice cocktail
1 12-ounce can ginger ale or lemon lime soda
1 6-ounce can frozen lemonade concentrate
8 ounces bourbon
Orange peel twists

*

Combine all the ingredients except orange peel and place in a freezer-safe container. Cover and freeze. Allow to thaw for 10 minutes before serving. Spoon the slushy mixture into glasses. Garnish with the orange peel twists. Store leftovers in the freezer.

*Serves 6 to 8.*

> **"We gave him an unlimited expense account and he's already exceeded it."**
>
> Redskins owner Edward Bennett Williams commenting on George Allen

Based on a traditional red wine punch and popular in Europe for hundreds of years, Sangria was introduced to Americans during the 1964 World's Fair. The punch base is typically Bordeaux wine, with brandy and fruit added for flavor. This drink pairs well with grilled food.

---

# Red Sangria

1 bottle (750 ml) dry red wine
½ cup fresh orange juice
¼ cup fresh lime juice
¼ cup Grand Marnier or brandy
½ cup granulated sugar

*

Peel the oranges and limes and cut the peels into very thin strips, removing the white pith. In a large pitcher, stir together the wine, juices, and Grand Marnier or brandy. Add the sugar, stir to dissolve, and chill overnight.

Just before serving, add the reserved peels to the pitcher. Serve in wine glasses, over ice.

*Makes 8½ cups.*

> **"It's not whether you get knocked down, it's whether you get up."**
>
> Vince Lombardi

We believe in equal opportunity, and that goes for our wine too. We therefore include a white wine version of the Sangria our guests love so much with grilled fare. This drink pairs well with chicken and fish.

---

# Sangria Blanco

3 cups dry white wine
¼ cup Grand Marnier
1 peach, sliced
1 orange, sliced
2 nectarines, sliced
2 lemons, sliced
2 limes, sliced
10 ounces Bitter Lemon

 &ast;

Mix the wine, Grand Marnier, and fruits together in a pitcher. Chill overnight. At serving time, add the Bitter Lemon and serve over ice.

*Serves 4 to 6.*

This special treat also doubles as a dessert after the *Monday Night Football* game. Warm dark chocolate is combined with coffee-flavored liqueur and topped off with whipped cream. Make enough for the whole family and pour the kids' portions before you add the Kahlua.

## Spiked Hot Chocolate

6 ounces dark chocolate

4 cups whole milk

½ cup Kahlua

⅓ cup whipping cream, whipped

Cocoa powder

＊

In a large saucepan, over medium heat, combine the chocolate and milk and stir until the chocolate is melted. Add the Kahlua and whisk until the mixture is hot.

Remove the mixture from the heat and pour into mugs. Top with the whipped cream and sprinkle with cocoa powder.

*Serves 6.*

> **"The definition of an atheist in Alabama is a person who doesn't believe in Bear Bryant."**
>
> University of Georgia Athletic Director Wally Butts

## A Case of Great Beers

If you've decided that beer really is your football beverage of choice, you're not alone. The United States currently produces 210,078,000 barrels of beer each year and, according to the Brewers Association, supports more breweries than all of Germany. We've taken our favorite 24 quaffs and assigned them to their respective league. Enjoy!

National Football Conference

Abita Turbodog, Abita Brewing Company, Abita Springs, Louisiana

Alaskan Amber Ale, Alaskan Brewing Company, Juneau

American Amber Ale, Rogue Ales, Newport, Oregon

August Schell Pilsner, August Schell Brewing Company, New Ulm, Minnesota

Hefe Weiss, Sprecher Brewing Company, Milwaukee

Honkers Ale, Goose Island Brewing Company, Chicago

Mirror Pond Pale Ale, Deschutes Brewing Company, Bend, Oregon

Prima Pils, Victory Brewing Company, Downington, Pennsylvania

Racer 5 India Pale Ale, Bear Republic Brewing Company, Healdsburg, California

Saint Arnold Amber, Saint Arnold Brewing Company, Houston

Summit Extra Pale Ale, Summit Brewing Company, St. Paul

Weizen, Widmer Brother Brewing Company, Portland, Oregon

American Football Conference

Alpha King Pale Ale, Three Floyds Brewing Company, Hammond, Indiana

Avery IPA, Avery Brewing Company, Boulder, Colorado

Bell's Amber Ale, Kalamazoo Brewing Company, Kalamazoo, Michigan

Boulevard Pale Ale, Boulevard Brewing Company, Kansas
City, Missouri

Brooklyn Lager, Brooklyn Brewery, Brooklyn

Dortmunder Gold Lager, Great Lakes Brewing Company,
Cleveland, Ohio

Export Ale, Shipyard Brewing Company, Portland, Maine

Harpoon India Pale Ale, Harpoon Brewing Company,
Boston

Jinx, Magic Hat Brewing Company, Burlington, Vermont

Odell's 90 Shilling, Odell Brewing Company, Fort Collins,
Colorado

Single Track Copper Ale, Boulder Beer Company, Boulder,
Colorado

Stone Pale Ale, Stone Brewing Company, San Diego,
California

# Team Efforts

## Menus for Every Setting

Every now and again, a little bit of magic happens and a group of talented players find themselves on the same team, and the coach of that team skillfully designs his strategy around the players' strengths and weaknesses. The team goes out and wins great games and the momentum builds, and the team rolls into the next year and keeps on winning, and the next thing you know, you have a football dynasty.

These dynasties all share two things in common. For a moment in time every player clicked, each understood his part in the magic, and a coach who knew how to show them the way led the team to victory.

### Green Bay Packers, 1960–1967

Vince Lombardi's Green Bay Packers won five NFL titles between 1961 and 1967, including the infamous Ice Bowl and Super Bowls I and II. The team boasts 12 Hall of Fame inductees and lost only 20 games in seven years.

> "The quality of a man's life is in direct proportion to his commitment to excellence, regardless of his chosen field of endeavor."
>
> Vince Lombardi

> "When he said sit down, I didn't even bother to look for a chair."
>
> Packers wide receiver Max McGee

## Miami Dolphins, 1971–1974

The Miami Dolphins set the standard for excellence in 1972, executing the only undefeated season in NFL history, 17–0. With Don Shula coaching men who are now football legends—Larry Csonka, Mercury Morris, Paul Warfield, and the great Bob Griese—they made three Super Bowl appearances in three years, winning the Lombardi trophy in 1972 and 1973.

> "I don't know any other way to lead but by example."
> Don Shula

> "If a nuclear bomb is dropped on this country, the only thing I'm sure will survive will be AstroTurf and Don Shula."
> Bubba Smith

## Pittsburgh Steelers, 1974–1979

Between 1974 and 1979, the Pittsburgh Steelers won four Super Bowls—the first team to do so—and today, ten of those players have been inducted into the Hall of Fame, including Terry Bradshaw, Lynn Swann, and "Mean" Joe Green. The team's impenetrable defense, the "Steel Curtain," dominated the AFC Central Division six years in a row.

> "We consider our Super Bowl trophy an antique."
> Chuck Noll, on Opening Day, after winning the Super Bowl the previous year

> "They can put on my tombstone: 'He'd 'a' lasted a lot longer if he hadn't played Pittsburgh six times in two years.'"
> Oilers coach Bum Phillips

## San Francisco Forty-Niners, 1981–1989

In 1981 the fairy dust was sprinkled over Candlestick Park when innovative coach Bill Walsh brought together quarterback Joe Montana, wide receiver Jerry Rice, John Taylor, Dwight Clark, Roger Craig, and a host of other talented players. Their winning streak would last until 1989 and included four Super Bowl wins.

> "If Bill Walsh was a general, he would be able to overrun Europe with the army from Sweden."
> Beano Cook

> "I don't know if he'll be there with us in the Hall of Fame. Hell, they might have to build this boy his own wing."
> Sammy Baugh, on Joe Montana

A great menu is a group of talented dishes that come together and become more than the sum of their parts. They work as a team in flavor, texture, color, and timing to provide your guests with an experience that satiates the hunger and excites the senses. This chapter gives you a game plan for success. We've carefully coordinated these special teams to make sure you can watch the game and still put on a winning cooking performance. Suit up!

There are few things more exciting for the serious fan than the first exhibition game of the season. Off-season is officially over, and we like to celebrate with some classic summer foods. This menu lets you entertain your guests casually while still catching a glimpse of this season's rookies.

---

## Pre-Season Exhibition Game

Goal Line Guacamole
Caramelized Onion Dip
Selection of Regional Beers
Halftime Beer Burgers
Hot Dogs
Leta B's Coleslaw
Potato Salad
Texas Baked Beans
Chocolate Zucchini Cake

## THE DAY BEFORE THE GAME

Make Caramelized Onion Dip; refrigerate

Make beef patties; refrigerate

Make Leta B's Coleslaw; refrigerate

Boil potatoes for Potato Salad; refrigerate

Prepare Texas Baked Beans up to point of baking; cover
    and refrigerate

Make Chocolate Zucchini Cake

## GAME DAY

*Before the First Quarter*

Assemble the Potato Salad; refrigerate

*Just before Kick-Off*

Make Goal Line Guacamole and serve with tortilla chips

Serve Caramelized Onion Dip with chips

*Late in the First Quarter*

Put Texas Baked Beans in oven

*Halftime*

Grill the burgers and hot dogs

Assemble the burgers and serve

Serve the Coleslaw, Potato Salad and Texas Baked Beans

*Last Commercial Break of Third Quarter*

Slice Chocolate Zucchini Cake

The regular season has started and life returns to normal for millions of football fans. Hope springs eternal, and so far no one is on the injured list, so we like to invite friends over to enjoy the game and the possibility of a great season!

# Season Kick-Off Game

Mojitos
Red Zone Layered Dip
Grilled Scotch Salmon
Corn Soufflé
Gridiron Green Bean Salad
Raspberry Oatmeal Bars

## THE DAY BEFORE THE GAME

Make Red Zone Layered Dip; refrigerate
Make Raspberry Oatmeal Bars; cool and cover
Prepare beans for Gridiron Green Bean Salad; refrigerate
Make dressing for Green Bean Salad; cover and refrigerate

## GAME DAY

### Before Guests Arrive

Assemble the Corn Soufflé
Marinate salmon

### Just before Kick-Off

Make Mojitos
Serve Red Zone Layered Dip with tortilla chips
Bake the Corn Soufflé

### Halftime

Grill the salmon; slice and serve
Assemble the Green Bean Salad and serve
Serve the Corn Soufflé

### Late in the Third Quarter

Serve Raspberry Oatmeal Bars

Tailgating is now a national phenomenon enjoyed by fans of every sport, including NASCAR. All tailgate parties need food that travels well and doesn't require last minute fussing at the stadium. This menu is one of our favorites.

# Tailgate Party

Roasted Red Pepper Dip
Chili Chaser Soup
Onion-Cheddar Corn Bread
Almond Taffy Bars

## TWO DAYS BEFORE THE GAME

Make Roasted Red Pepper Dip; refrigerate

## THE DAY BEFORE THE GAME

Make Chili Chaser Soup; refrigerate
Prepare Onion-Cheddar Corn Bread up to point of baking;
    cover and refrigerate
Bake Almond Taffy Bars

## GAME DAY

### Before You Leave

Bake corn bread; while still warm, cover with aluminum
    foil and place in cooler lined with newspaper
Reheat the soup and transport in wide-mouth thermos
Slice Almond Taffy Bars

### At the Stadium

Serve Roasted Red Pepper Dip
Cut corn bread and allow tailgaters to help themselves
    with a spatula
Serve soup in sturdy plastic bowls
Serve Almond Taffy Bars on a serving plate

The University of Illinois claims to have held the first Homecoming in October 1910. Now a college tradition, Homecoming weekend welcomes alumni back to their alma mater for a reunion and—everyone hopes—a great football game. This menu lets you do all the preparation in advance so that you're free to reminisce with friends.

---

# Homecoming Weekend Game

Coin Toss Cheese Crisps
Red Sangria
Muffaletta Tailgater
Butternut Squash and Apple Soup
Black Walnut and Butterscotch Cookies

## THE DAY BEFORE THE GAME

Make Sangria; refrigerate

Make Coin Toss Cheese Crisps and keep in airtight container

Make Muffaletta Tailgater sandwich; refrigerate

Make Butternut Squash and Apple Soup; refrigerate

Make Black Walnut and Butterscotch Cookies

## GAME DAY

### *Before Leaving for the Game*

Put Sangria in a thermos

Wrap Muffaletta Tailgater in foil

Gently reheat the soup; transport in thermos

### *At the Tailgate*

Serve cheese crisps on a serving plate

Slice Muffaletta Tailgater

Offer soup in small plastic bowls or mugs

Place cookies on a serving plate

*Monday Night Football* aired its first game on September 21, 1970, and became one of the most successful shows in broadcast history. Through the skilled commentary of football greats like Frank Gifford, Al Michaels, and the unforgettable John Madden, we developed a new understanding of the game. This menu guarantees you can sit back and enjoy a great meal without missing the action.

## Monday Night Football Game

Chilled Shrimp with Classic Shrimp Cocktail Sauce
Regional Beer
Meatloaf Sandwiches with Blue Cheese Dressing
Cheesy Potato Casserole
Green Salad
Cinnamon Chocolate Chip Cookies

## TWO DAYS BEFORE THE GAME

Make Classic Shrimp Cocktail Sauce; refrigerate

## THE DAY BEFORE THE GAME

Make meatloaf; cool and refrigerate
Make Blue Cheese Dressing; refrigerate
Buy peeled, deveined shrimp or the precooked variety
Make Cinnamon Chocolate Chip Cookies; keep in airtight
    container

## GAME DAY

### Before the Pregame Show

Cook, cool and refrigerate shrimp
Prepare Cheesy Potato Casserole
Gently reheat the meatloaf in oven
Prepare salad ingredients and dressing of your choice;
    keep separate

### Just before Kick-Off

Serve shrimp with cocktail sauce
Put Cheesy Potato Casserole in oven

### Halftime

Slice meatloaf and serve on buns with Blue Cheese
    Dressing
Toss salad with dressing of your choice and serve
Serve Cheesy Potato Casserole

### Third Quarter

Set cookies out

The Army-Navy game pits the football teams of the United States Military Academy at West Point against the United States Naval Academy at Annapolis on the last weekend of the regular season. The game is broadcast to service installations worldwide. It's one of the most enduring rivalries in college football history and has featured five Heisman trophy winners. Instant replay made its debut during the 1963 Army-Navy game. We like to honor the tradition with this All-American menu.

## The Army-Navy Game

Baked Buffalo Wings
Regional Beers
Philly Cheese Steak Sandwiches
Potato Salad
Point After Peanut Butter Cookies

## THE DAY BEFORE THE GAME

Boil potatoes for Potato Salad; cool and refrigerate in covered container

Make the cookies; cool and keep in airtight container

## GAME DAY

### Before the Game

Prepare the Baked Buffalo Wings up to point of baking and keep refrigerated

Make the Potato Salad and refrigerate

### Before Kick-Off

Bake the chicken wings and serve with blue cheese sauce at kick-off

Cook the vegetables for the Philly Cheese Steak Sandwiches up to point of adding beef and remove from heat

### Halftime

Finish the Philly Cheese Steak Sandwiches and serve with Potato Salad on the side.

### First Commercial Break in the Fourth Quarter

Serve the cookies

In the 1970s, professional football became the most popular sport in America, and the NFL responded by increasing the number of franchises and offering a doubleheader on Sundays. We are eternally grateful because we can now enjoy our two favorite things at once—brunch and football! This menu keeps you out of the kitchen until halftime and always gets rave reviews.

## Sunday Brunch for the Early Game

Hot Crab Quesadillas
Bloody Hail Mary
Cheese Strata
Glazed Sausage and Apples
RJ's Hash Browns
Cinnamon Chocolate Chip Cookies

## THE DAY BEFORE THE GAME

Boil potatoes, cool, dice and refrigerate

Make Cheese Strata up to point of baking; cover and
    refrigerate

Make Cinnamon Chocolate Chip Cookies

## GAME DAY

### *Before the Game*

Brown the sausage; drain and cool

Assemble quesadilla ingredients

### *Just before Kick-Off*

Make Bloody Hail Marys

Put Cheese Strata in oven

Make Hot Crab Quesadillas and serve

### *Commercial Break in Second Quarter*

Chop onions for hash browns

Take potatoes out of refrigerator to return to room
    temperature

### *Halftime*

Fry the hash browns

Finish Glazed Sausage and Apples and serve

Serve Cheese Strata

### *Last Commercial Break of Third Quarter*

Serve Cinnamon Chocolate Chip Cookies

Long before professional football hit prime time television, the NFL struggled to get the sport on the air. Working with CBS, Commissioner Bert Bell inked a deal to broadcast each team's away games on Sunday—a time slot previously difficult to program. So began the tradition of Sunday games, and this classic comfort food menu is a great choice for the game.

## Sunday Dinner Game

Melissa's Artichoke Dip
Bull Shots
Lasagna
Roasted Garlic Bread
Green Salad
Pumpkin Bread

## THE DAY BEFORE THE GAME

Make All-Pro Tomato-Meat Sauce; cover and refrigerate
Make ricotta cheese mixture for Lasagna; cover and
  refrigerate
Make Pumpkin Bread
Prepare the spread for the Roasted Garlic Bread; cover and
refrigerate

## GAME DAY

### *Before the Pregame Show*

Make Melissa's Artichoke Dip and bake
Assemble the Lasagna

### *Before Kick-Off*

Put Lasagna in to bake
Spread the roasted garlic on split Italian bread
Wash salad greens and prepare dressing of your choice
Make Bull Shots

### *Halftime*

Toast garlic bread
Toss salad with dressing and serve with the Lasagna

### *Third Quarter Commercial Break*

Serve Pumpkin Bread

If your team has managed to get into the playoffs, the last place you want to be during the game is in the kitchen. This simple menu offers great recipes that work around the gridiron action, leaving you free to scream at the referees.

---

# Semi-Final Playoff Game

Honey Mustard Chicken Drumettes
Whiskey Sours
Midfield Mac and Cheese
Roasted Garlic Bread
Green Salad
Merlot Brownies

## THE DAY BEFORE THE GAME

Marinate chicken drumettes
Prepare Midfield Mac and Cheese up to point of baking;
    cover with aluminum foil and refrigerate
Prepare the spread for Roasted Garlic Bread; refrigerate
Make brownies

## GAME DAY

### Just before the Pregame Show

Put Honey Mustard Chicken Drumettes in oven
Spread the roasted garlic on split Italian bread
Wash salad greens and prepare dressing of choice

### Just before Kick-Off

Put Midfield Mac and Cheese in oven
Make Whiskey Sours
Serve drumettes

### Halftime

Toast the garlic bread
Serve Midfield Mac and Cheese
Dress and serve salad

### Late in the Third Quarter

Serve brownies

The Rose Bowl—originally titled the "Tournament East-West" football game—was first played on January 1, 1902. The inaugural game pitted a dominant Michigan team against Stanford University, with a final score of 49–0. The game was so lopsided that Tournament of Roses officials decided to run chariot races, ostrich races, and other events instead. But on New Year's Day in 1916, football returned to the tournament and is now a tradition for millions of college football fans. If you're one of them, this menu is for you.

---

# New Year's Day College Bowl Celebration

Coin Toss Cheese Crisps
Chilled Shrimp with Triple Citrus Thai Chili Sauce
Bloody Hail Marys
Chile Rellenos Strata
Cinnamon Crunch Coffee Cake
Fruit Platter
Chocolate Chip Crunch Cookies
Tailgate Toffee

## THE DAY BEFORE THE GAME

Make Coin Toss Cheese Crisps; keep in airtight container
Make Triple Citrus Thai Chili Sauce; cover and refrigerate
Make the coffee cake
Make the cookies and Tailgate Toffee
Buy peeled and deveined shrimp or the precooked variety

## GAME DAY

*Before the Game*

Assemble the Chile Rellenos Strata
Cook and chill shrimp
Prepare a platter of favorite fruits; cover and refrigerate
Mix the Bloody Hail Marys

*During the Pregame Show*

Serve the Bloody Hail Marys with the Cheese Crisps and
    shrimp with dipping sauce

*Just before Kick-Off*

Put the strata in oven to bake

*Halftime*

Serve the strata with your favorite salsa and fruit platter
Cut and serve the coffee cake

*Between the Third and Fourth Quarters*

Serve Chocolate Chip Crunch Cookies and Tailgate Toffee

Now an unofficial national holiday, Super Bowl day draws an esti-
mated billion people worldwide to watch the game. Friends and family who haven't watched football all year come out of the woodwork
to enjoy the show, including the commercials. This menu is heavy on
finger food and designed to keep the host watching the NFC-AFC
matchup, not the stove.

# Super Bowl Sunday

Classic Potato Skins
The Fearsome Threesome
Our Favorite Nachos
Black Bean Salsa
Margaritas
Liberty Street Chili
Corn Muffins
Everything-but-the-Kitchen-Sink Cookies
Excessive Celebration Peanut Butter Brownies

## TWO DAYS BEFORE THE GAME

Bake potatoes for Classic Potato Skins
Cook bacon for potato skins; keep in plastic bag
Make cookies; keep in airtight container
Make brownies; cool and cover

## THE DAY BEFORE THE GAME

Make Fearsome Threesome dips; refrigerate
Make Liberty Street Chili; cool and refrigerate
Make or buy the Corn Muffins

## GAME DAY

*Before the Game*

Make Black Bean Salsa
Prepare nachos to point of baking
Assemble and bake the potato skins

*During Pregame Show*

Make Margaritas
Serve Fearsome Threesome dips with chips/vegetables
Serve Classic Potato Skins

*Commercial Break during First Quarter*

Bake nachos

*Second Quarter*

Set out salsa
Serve nachos
Gently reheat the chili

*Halftime*

Serve chili with optional toppings and corn muffins on the
    side.

*Late in Third Quarter*

Serve brownies and cookies on a platter

The inaugural Pro Bowl was played on January 15, 1930, pitting the NFL champions against an all-star team from the rest of the league. Since the merger of the American Football League and the NFL in 1967, the game has been played by all-stars from each conference. Sadly, it also marks the beginning of the off-season. It will be five long months before the first exhibition game is played—so enjoy!

## All The Way to the Pro-Bowl

Spicy Cocktail Nuts
Braised Short Ribs
Cheese Biscuits
Roasted Sweet Potatoes and Onions
Caramel Apple Pie

## THE DAY BEFORE THE GAME

Make the Spicy Cocktail Nuts; keep in airtight container
Make the Caramel Apple Pie; cool and cover
Make the Cheese Biscuits
Make the Roasted Sweet Potatoes and Onions; cool, cover
    and refrigerate

## GAME DAY

*Before the Game*

Prepare the Braised Short Ribs and bake

*Just before Kick-Off*

Serve the Spicy Cocktail Nuts

*End of First Quarter*

Put the Roasted Sweet Potatoes and Onions in the oven,
    covered, and gently reheat

*Halftime*

Serve Braised Short Ribs with Cheese Biscuits on the side
    and the Roasted Sweet Potatoes and Onions

*First Commercial Break in the Fourth Quarter*

Cut and serve the Caramel Apple Pie

# Index

After Thanksgiving Day Sandwich, 61
Allen, George, 165
All-Pro Tomato-Meat Sauce, 89
Almond Taffy Bars, 136
American Tailgaters Association, xi, 52
Appetizers:
    Baked Buffalo Wings, 19
    Barbecue Cocktail Riblets, 21
    Beef Kabobs with Hoisin Marinade, 39
    Black Bean Salsa, 24
    Chili Con Queso, 26
    Classic Potato Skins, 22
    Classic Shrimp Cocktail Sauce, 6
    Coin Toss Cheese Crisps, 15
    Double Team Shrimp, 94
    The Fearsome Threesome, 13
    First Round Draft Deviled Eggs, 16
    Goal Line Guacamole, 9
    Herbed Cheese, 27
    Honey Mustard Chicken Drumettes, 23
    Hot Crab Quesadillas, 74
    Melissa's Artichoke Dip, 10
    No Chop Salsa, 25
    Our Favorite Nachos, 17
    Red Zone Layered Dip, 11
    Roasted Red Pepper Dip, 12
    Salsa Cream Sauce, 8
    Smoky Chip Dip, 13
    Spicy Cocktail Nuts, 18
    Triple Citrus Thai Chili Sauce, 7
Apples:
    Apple Cinnamon Dutch Baby, 73
    Apple Pandowdy, 149
    Butternut Squash and Apple Soup, 100
    Caramel Apple Pie, 150
    Glazed Sausage and Apples, 78
Arbanas, Fred, 121
Arena Football, 154–55

Arledge, Roone, 114
Army-Navy Game, 182
Artichokes:
    Melissa's Artichoke Dip, 10
Auntie Fran's Baby Back Ribs, 96
Avocados:
    Goal Line Guacamole, 9

Bacon, Glazed, 79
Baked Buffalo Wings, 19
Baked Eggs, 68
Barbecue:
    Auntie Fran's Baby Back Ribs, 96
    Barbecue Cocktail Riblets, 21
    Quick Kick Barbecue Sauce, 51
Barry, Dave, 87
Bars:
    Almond Taffy Bars, 136
    Raspberry Oatmeal Bars, 135
Baugh, Sammy, 173
Beans:
    Black Bean Salsa, 24
    Gridiron Green Bean Salad, 130
    Liberty Street Chili, 109
    Our Favorite Nachos, 17
    Red Zone Layered Dip, 11
    Texas Baked Beans, 116
Beef:
    All-Pro Tomato-Meat Sauce, 89
    Beef Kabobs with Hoisin Marinade, 39
    Braised Short Ribs, 97
    Halftime Beer Burgers, 40
    Liberty Street Chili, 109
    Meatloaf Sandwiches with Blue Cheese Dressing, 58
    Our Favorite Sloppy Joes, 65
    Philly Cheese Steak Sandwiches, 60
    Rib Eye Steaks with Salsa, 37
    Steak Bites with Remoulade Sauce, 35
    Texas Beef Chili, 110

Beer:
  Beer Brats, 50
  Beer Can Chicken, 48
  Halftime Beer Burgers, 40
  regional beers, 169
Bell, Bert, 67
Bell, Tommy, 121
Beverages:
  Bloody Hail Mary, 158
  Bourbon Slush, 164
  Bull Shot, 159
  Mango Margaritas, 162
  Margaritas, 163
  Mojito, 160
  Red Dunebuggy, 165
  Red Sangria, 166
  regional beers, 169
  Sangria Blanco, 167
  Spiked Hot Chocolate, 168
  Whiskey Sours over Ice, 161
Bevo, 80
Bicknell, Jack, 133
Biscuits, Cheese, 118
Black Bean Salsa, 24
Black Walnut and Butterscotch Cookies,
  145
Bloody Hail Mary, 158
Bombeck, Erma, 61
Bourbon:
  Bourbon Slush, 164
  Red Dunebuggy, 165
Bradshaw, Terry, 99, 134, 172
Braised Short Ribs, 97
Bratwurst:
  Beer Brats, 50
Bratzke, Chad, 101
Breads:
  Cheddar Cheese Toasts, 117
  Cheese Biscuits, 118
  Corn Muffins, 120
  Onion-Cheddar Corn Bread, 121
  Pumpkin Bread, 146
  Roasted Garlic Bread, 122
Brown, Heywood Hale, 126
Brownies:
  Excessive Celebration Peanut Butter
    Brownies, 137
  Merlot Brownies, 139

Brunch, 67
  Apple Cinnamon Dutch Baby, 73
  Baked Eggs, 68
  Caramel French Toast, 72
  Cheese Strata, 69
  Chili Rellenos Strata, 70
  Cinnamon Crunch Coffee Cake, 75
  Glazed Bacon, 79
  Glazed Sausage and Apples, 78
  Hot Crab Quesadillas, 74
  menu, 184
  RJ's Hash Browns, 77
Bryant, Bear, 168
Buffalo Chicken Salad, 82
Bull Shot, 159
Buoniconti, Nick, 40
Burritos:
  Chili Verde Burritos, 66
  Mexican Salad Burritos, 127
Butkus, Dick, 73, 157
Buttermilk:
  Maili's Buttermilk Fried Chicken, 86
Butternut Squash and Apple Soup,
  100
Butterscotch:
  Black Walnut and Butterscotch
    Cookies, 145
Butts, Wally, 168

Cabbage:
  Leta B's Coleslaw, 132
Cakes:
  Chocolate Zucchini Cake, 148
  Cinnamon Crunch Coffee Cake, 75
Caramel:
  Caramel Apple Pie, 150
  Caramel French Toast, 72
Casseroles:
  Cheese Strata, 69
  Cheesy Potato Casserole, 124
  Chile Rellenos Strata, 70
  Lasagna, 91
Cheddar Cheese Toasts, 117
Cheese:
  Cheddar Cheese Toasts, 117
  Cheese Biscuits, 118
  Cheese Strata, 69
  Cheesy Potato Casserole, 124

Chile Rellenos Strata, 70
Chili Con Queso, 26
Coin Toss Cheese Crisps, 15
Herbed Cheese, 27
Maili's Blue Cheese Dressing, 82
Meatloaf Sandwich Blue Cheese
    Dressing, 58
Midfield Mac and Cheese, 88
Onion-Cheddar Corn Bread, 121
Our Favorite Nachos, 17
Chicken:
    Baked Buffalo Wings, 19
    Beer Can Chicken, 48
    Buffalo Chicken Salad, 82
    Cider-Stewed Chicken, 107
    Cinnamon Rosemary Chicken, 47
    Cornmeal Crusted Chicken, 85
    Curried Chicken Pasta Salad, 128
    Dried Cranberry and Pecan
        Chicken Salad, 84
    Honey Mustard Chicken Drum-
        ettes, 23
    Maili's Buttermilk Fried Chicken, 86
Chiles:
    Chile Rellenos Strata, 70
    Chili Verde Burritos, 66
    Triple Citrus Thai Chili Sauce, 7
Chilis:
    Chili Chaser Soup, 101
    Chili Con Queso, 26
    Liberty Street Chili, 109
    Texas Beef Chili, 110
Chocolate:
    Chocolate Chip Crunch Cookies,
        143
    Chocolate Zucchini Cake, 148
    Cinnamon Chocolate Chip Cookies,
        140
    Spiked Hot Chocolate, 168
Chowder, Classic New England Clam,
    104
Cider-Stewed Chicken, 107
Cinnamon:
    Apple Cinnamon Dutch Baby, 73
    Cinnamon Chocolate Chip Cookies,
        140
    Cinnamon Crunch Coffee Cake, 75
    Cinnamon Rosemary Chicken, 47

Cioppino, Fisherman's Wharf, 105
Clams:
    Clam Dip, 14
    Classic New England Clam Chow-
        der, 104
Clark, Dwight, 173
Classic New England Clam Chowder,
    104
Classic Potato Skins, 22
Classic Reuben, The, 62
Classic Shrimp Cocktail Sauce, 6
Coffee Cake, Cinnamon Crunch, 75
Coin Toss Cheese Crisps, 15
Coleslaw, Leta B's, 132
Cook, Beano, 173
Cookies:
    Black Walnut and Butterscotch
        Cookies, 145
    Chocolate Chip Crunch Cookies,
        143
    Cinnamon Chocolate Chip Cookies,
        140
    Everything-but-the-Kitchen-Sink
        Cookies, 141
    Point After Peanut Butter Cookies,
        144
Corn:
    Corn Muffins, 120
    Corn Soufflé, 119
    Onion-Cheddar Corn Bread, 121
Corned Beef:
    Classic Reuben, The, 62
Cornmeal Crusted Chicken, 85
Cosell, Howard, 114
Coslet, Bruce, 129
Crab:
    Hot Crab Quesadillas, 74
Craig, Roger, 173
Cranberries:
    Dried Cranberry and Pecan
        Chicken Salad, 84
Creole, Shrimp, 113
Csonka, Larry, 40, 172
Cubano Sandwich, 63
Cunningham, Randall, 98
Curries:
    Curried Chicken Pasta Salad, 128
    Mulligatawny, 102

Defensive alignment, 29
Dempsey, Tom, 12
Devine, Dan, 46
Dips:
    Caramelized Onion Dip, 13
    Clam Dip, 14
    Goal Line Guacamole, 9
    Melissa's Artichoke Dip, 10
    Red Zone Layered Dip, 11
    Roasted Red Pepper Dip, 12
    Smoky Chip Dip, 13
Double Team Shrimp, 94
Dressings:
    Balsamic Vinaigrette, 130
    Honey-Lime Dressing, 127
    Maili's Blue Cheese Dressing, 82
    Meatloaf Sandwich Blue Cheese
        Dressing, 58
Dried Cranberry and Pecan Chicken
    Salad, 84
Durfee, Jim, 57
Dynasties, football, 171

Eggs:
    Baked Eggs, 68
    Cheese Strata, 69
    Chile Rellenos Strata, 70
    First Round Draft Deviled Eggs, 16
Elway, John, 133
Esiason, Boomer, 115
Everything-but-the-Kitchen-Sink
    Cookies, 141
Excessive Celebration Peanut Butter
    Brownies, 137

Fearsome Threesome, The, 13
First Round Draft Deviled Eggs, 16
Fish:
    Fisherman's Wharf Cioppino, 105
    Fish Tacos, 44
    Grilled Scotch Salmon, 46
Fisherman's Wharf Cioppino, 105
Fog Bowl, 99
Football movies, 155
French Bread Pizza, 93
French Toast, Caramel, 72
Fruit:
    Glazed Sausage and Apples, 78
    Mango Margaritas, 162

    Mango Salsa, 70
    Raspberry Oatmeal Bars, 135

Garlic:
    Roasted Garlic Bread, 122
Gifford, Frank, 114–15
Glazed Bacon, 79
Glazed Sausage and Apples, 78
Goal Line Guacamole, 9
Grange, Red, 4
Granville, Gerry, 80
Green, Mean Joe, 172
Green, Tim, 36
Green Beans:
    Gridiron Green Bean Salad, 130
Gridiron basics, 28
Gridiron Green Bean Salad, 130
Griese, Bob, 40, 172
Griffen, Archie, 142
Grilling:
    Beef Kabobs with Hoisin Mari-
        nade, 39
    Beer Brats, 50
    Beer Can Chicken, 48
    Cinnamon Rosemary Chicken, 47
    Fish Tacos, 44
    Grilled Scotch Salmon, 46
    Grilled Souvlaki in Pita, 42
    Halftime Beer Burgers, 40
    Lamb Pinchitos, 41
    Rib Eye Steaks with Salsa, 37
    Steak Bites with Remoulade
        Sauce, 35
Guacamole, Goal Line, 9

Halas, George, 57, 90, 151
Halftime Beer Burgers, 40
Ham:
    Cubano Sandwich, 63
Hamburgers:
    Halftime Beer Burgers, 40
Harmon, Mark, 133
Harris, Franco, 134
Hash Browns, RJ's, 77
Heffelfinger, William, 159
Heisman, John, 140
Herbed Cheese, 27
Hilgenberg, Jay, 99
Holtz, Lou, 138

Holub, E. J., 161
Homecoming, xi, 178
Honey:
    Honey-Lime Dressing, 127
    Honey Mustard Chicken Drum-
        ettes, 23
Hot Crab Quesadillas, 74

Ice Bowl, 92, 98, 108, 171
Immaculate Reception, 134

Jackson, Keith, 114

Karras, Alex, 115
Keislung, Walt, 79
Kemp, Jack, 147
Kiick, Jim, 40

Lamb:
    Grilled Souvlaki in Pita, 42
    Lamb Pinchitos, 41
Landry, Tom, 80, 102, 135
Lasagna, 91
Leta B's Coleslaw, 132
Liberty Street Chili, 109
Lime:
    Honey-Lime Dressing, 127
Lombardi, Vince, 8, 38, 80, 81, 166, 171
Looney, Joe Don, 80

Macaroni Salad, 129
Madden, John, 20, 115, 157
Maili's Buttermilk Fried Chicken, 86
Mango:
    Mango Margaritas, 162
    Mango Salsa, 70
Margaritas:
    Mango Margaritas, 162
    Margaritas, 163
Marinade, Hoisin, 39
McGee, Max, 171
McKay, John, 103
Meatloaf Sandwich with Blue Cheese
    Dressing, 58
Melissa's Artichoke Dip, 10
Menus:
    All the Way to the Pro Bowl, 194
    Army-Navy Game, 182
    Homecoming Weekend, 178

Monday Night Football, 180
    New Year's Day College Bowl Cele-
        bration, 190
    Pre-Season Exhibition, 174
    Season Kick-Off, 176
    Semi-Final Playoff, 188
    Sunday Brunch for the Early Game,
        184
    Sunday Dinner Game, 186
    Super Bowl Sunday, 192
    Tailgate Party, 177
Meredith, Don, 114
Merlot Brownies, 139
Mexican Salad Burritos, 127
Michaels, Al, 115
Michaels, Walt, 117
Midfield Mac and Cheese, 88
Millen, Matt, 14
Miller, Dennis, 115
Moen, Kevin, 133
Mojitos, 160
*Monday Night Football*, xi, 55, 114–15,
    154, 157
Monday Night Football menu, 180
Montana, Joe, 173
Morris, Mercury, 172
Movies, football, 155
Muffaletta Tailgater, 56
Muffins, Corn, 120
Mulligatawny, 102

Nachos, Our Favorite, 17
Nagurski, Bronco, 4
Namath, Joe, 115, 157
Neale, Greasy, 79
New Year's Day College Bowl Celebra-
    tion menu, 190
No-Chop Salsa, 25
Noll, Chuck, 172
Nuts:
    Almond Taffy Bars, 136
    Black Walnut and Butterscotch
        Cookies, 145
    Spicy Cocktail Nuts, 18

Oatmeal:
    Raspberry Oatmeal Bars, 135
Offensive formation, 29
Off-season, 154

Onions:
  Caramelized Onion Dip, 13
  Onion-Cheddar Corn Bread, 121
  Roasted Sweet Potatoes and Onions,
    125
Our Favorite Nachos, 17
Our Favorite Sloppy Joes, 65

Pasta:
  Curried Chicken Pasta Salad, 128
  Lasagna, 91
  Macaroni Salad, 129
  Midfield Mac and Cheese, 88
Peanut Butter:
  Excessive Celebration Peanut Butter
    Brownies, 137
  Point After Peanut Butter Cookies,
    144
Pearson, Drew, 133
Pecans:
  Dried Cranberry and Pecan
    Chicken Salad, 84
Penalties, 31
Peppers:
  Roasted Red Pepper Dip, 12
Phillips, Bum, 172
Philly Cheese Steak Sandwiches, 60
Pie, Caramel Apple, 150
Pigskin Pulled Pork, 95
Pizza, French Bread, 93
Players, definition of, 29–30
Point After Peanut Butter Cookies, 144
Pork:
  Auntie Fran's Baby Back Ribs, 96
  Barbecue Cocktail Riblets, 21
  Chili Verde Burritos, 66
  Cubano Sandwiches, 63
  Pigskin Pulled Pork, 95
  Pork Picadillo, 111
Potatoes:
  Cheesy Potato Casserole, 124
  Classic Potato Skins, 22
  Potato Salad, 123
  RJ's Hash Browns, 77
  Roasted Sweet Potatoes and Onions,
    125
Potter, Stephen, ix
Pro-Bowl menu, 194
Pumpkin Bread, 146

Quesadillas, Hot Crab, 74
Quick Kick Barbecue Sauce, 51

Raspberry Oatmeal Bars, 135
Raveling, George, 165
Red Dunebuggy, 165
Red Sangria, 166
Red Zone, 9, 31
Red Zone Layered Dip, 11
Rentzel, Lance, 92, 98
Rib Eye Steaks with Salsa, 37
Ribs:
  Auntie Fran's Baby Back Ribs, 96
  Barbecue Cocktail Riblets, 21
  Braised Short Ribs, 97
Rice, Jerry, 173
Richards, George, 93
Riggs, Gerald, 18
RJ's Hash Browns, 77
Roasted Fall Vegetables, 126
Roasted Garlic Bread, 122
Roasted Red Pepper Dip, 12
Roasted Sweet Potatoes and Onions, 125
Rockne, Knute, 68
Rose Bowl, 190
Rote, Kyle, 1
Rozelle, Pete, 114
Rum:
  Mojito, 160

Salads:
  Buffalo Chicken Salad, 82
  Curried Chicken Pasta Salad, 128
  Dried Cranberry and Pecan
    Chicken Salad, 84
  Gridiron Green Bean Salad, 130
  Macaroni Salad, 129
  Mexican Salad Burritos, 127
  Potato Salad, 123
Salmon, Grilled Scotch, 46
Salsas:
  Black Bean Salsa, 24
  Mango Salsa, 70
  No-Chop Salsa, 25
  Pico de Gallo, 44
  Rib Eye Steaks with Salsa, 37
  Salsa Cream Sauce, 8
Sandwiches, 55
  After Thanksgiving Day Sandwich, 61

Chili Verde Burritos, 66
Classic Reuben, 62
Cubano Sandwich, 63
Meatloaf Sandwich with Blue
    Cheese Dressing, 58
Muffaletta Tailgater, 56
Our Favorite Sloppy Joes, 65
Philly Cheese Steak Sandwiches, 60
Sangrias:
    Red Sangria, 166
    Sangria Blanco, 167
Sauces:
    All-Pro Tomato-Meat Sauce, 89
    Baja Sauce, 44
    Classic Shrimp Cocktail Sauce, 6
    Quick Kick Barbecue Sauce, 51
    Remoulade Sauce, 35
    Salsa Cream Sauce, 8
    Triple Citrus Thai Chili Sauce, 7
    Yogurt Dill Sauce, 42
Sausage:
    All-Pro Tomato-Meat Sauce, 89
    Glazed Sausage and Apples, 78
    Red Zone Layered Dip, 11
Semi-Final Playoff Game menu, 188
Shankly, Bill, 125
Shrimp:
    Double Team Shrimp, 94
    Shrimp Creole, 113
Shula, Don, 172
Simpson, O. J., 115
Sloppy Joes, Our Favorite, 65
Smith, Bubba, 157, 172
Snell, Matt, 157
Snow Bowl, 98
Soufflé, Corn, 119
Soups:
    Butternut Squash and Apple Soup,
        100
    Chili Chaser Soup, 101
    Mulligatawny, 102
    Touchdown Tomato Soup, 103
Souvlaki:
    Grilled Souvlaki in Pita, 42
Spicy Cocktail Nuts, 18
Spiked Hot Chocolate, 168
Squash:
    Butternut Squash and Apple Soup,
        100

Starr, Bart, 123
Staubach, Roger, 133
Steak Bites with Remoulade Sauce, 35
Stews:
    Cider-Stewed Chicken, 107
    Fisherman's Wharf Cioppino, 105
Stratas:
    Cheese Strata, 69
    Chile Rellenos Strata, 70
Summerall, Pat, 1
Super Bowl, xi
Super Bowl Sunday menu, 192
Swann, Lynn, 172

Tacos, Fish, 44
Tailgate Party menu, 177
Tailgate recipes:
    Almond Taffy Bars, 136
    Beef Kabobs with Hoisin Mari-
        nade, 39
    Beer Brats, 50
    Black Bean Salsa, 24
    Black Walnut and Butterscotch
        Cookies, 145
    Chili Chaser Soup, 101
    Chocolate Chip Crunch Cookies, 143
    Chocolate Zucchini Cake, 148
    Cinnamon Chocolate Chip Cookies,
        140
    Cinnamon Rosemary Chicken, 47
    Coin Toss Cheese Crisps, 15
    Everything-but-the-Kitchen-Sink
        Cookies, 141
    Excessive Celebration Peanut Butter
        Brownies, 137
    The Fearsome Threesome, 13
    Fish Tacos, 44
    Goal Line Guacamole, 9
    Grilled Scotch Salmon, 46
    Grilled Souvlaki in Pita, 42
    Halftime Beer Burgers, 40
    Lamb Pinchitos, 41
    Lasagna, 91
    Liberty Street Chili, 109
    Merlot Brownies, 139
    Muffaletta Tailgater, 56
    Mulligatawny, 102
    Onion-Cheddar Corn Bread, 121
    Potato Salad, 123

Pumpkin Bread, 146
Raspberry Oatmeal Bars, 135
Red Zone Layered Dip, 11
Rib Eye Steaks with Salsa, 37
Roasted Red Pepper Dip, 11
Spicy Cocktail Nuts, 18
Steak Bites with Remoulade Sauce, 35
Tailgate Toffee, 152
Texas Baked Beans, 116
Texas Beef Chili, 110
Tailgating, 52–54
Tarkenton, Fran, 115
Taylor, John, 173
Taylor, Lionel, 151
Tequila:
    Mango Margaritas, 162
    Margaritas, 163
Texas Baked Beans, 116
Texas Beef Chili, 110
Thorpe, Jim, 4
Toffee, Tailgate, 152
Tomatoes:
    All-Pro Tomato-Meat Sauce, 89
    Touchdown Tomato Soup, 103
Tomczak, Mike, 98
Touchdown Tomato Soup, 103
Triple Citrus Thai Chili Sauce, 7
Turkey:
    After Thanksgiving Day Sandwich, 61

Unitas, Johnny, 1–2

Vegetarian:
    Almond Taffy Bars, 136
    Apple Cinnamon Dutch Baby, 73
    Apple Pandowdy, 149
    Black Bean Salsa, 24
    Black Walnut and Butterscotch
        Cookies, 145
    Caramel Apple Pie, 150
    Caramel French Toast, 72
    Cheddar Cheese Toasts, 117
    Cheese Biscuits, 118
    Cheesy Potato Casserole, 124
    Chili con Queso, 26
    Chile Rellenos Strata, 70
    Chocolate Chip Crunch Cookies, 143

Chocolate Zucchini Cake, 148
Cinnamon Chocolate Chip Cookies,
    140
Cinnamon Crunch Coffee Cake, 75
Coin Toss Cheese Crisps, 15
Corn Muffins, 120
Corn Soufflé, 119
Everything-but-the-Kitchen-Sink
    Cookies, 141
Excessive Celebration Peanut Butter
    Brownies, 137
First Round Draft Deviled Eggs, 16
Goal Line Guacamole, 9
Gridiron Green Bean Salad, 130
Herbed Cheese, 27
Leta B's Coleslaw, 132
Macaroni Salad, 129
Melissa's Artichoke Dip, 10
Merlot Brownies, 139
Mexican Salad Burritos, 127
Midfield Mac and Cheese, 88
No-Chop Salsa, 25
Onion-Cheddar Corn Bread, 121
Our Favorite Nachos, 17
Point After Peanut Butter Cookies,
    144
Potato Salad, 123
Pumpkin Bread, 146
Raspberry Oatmeal Bars, 135
RJ's Hash Browns, 77
Roasted Fall Vegetables, 126
Roasted Garlic Bread, 122
Roasted Red Pepper Dip, 12
Roasted Sweet Potatoes and Onions,
    125
Salsa Cream Sauce, 8
Spicy Cocktail Nuts, 18
Tailgate Toffee, 152
Vodka:
    Bloody Hail Mary, 158
    Bull Shot, 159

Walden, Jim, 77
Walsh, Bill, 173
Warfield, Paul, 40, 172
Whiskey Sours over Ice, 161
Williams, Edward Bennett, 165

Williams, Reggie, 95
Wine:
    Merlot Brownies, 139
    Red Sangria, 166
    Sangria Blanco, 167

Youngblood, Jack, 153

Zucchini:
    Chocolate Zucchini Cake, 148
Zuppke, Robert, 4

As a cooking instructor and lifelong football fan, Kellie Lawless develops recipes and party menus that are stress-free for the cook and fun for the fans. She is a Certified Kansas City Barbecue Judge, judging at dozens of barbecue competitions each year across the United States. Kellie lives in Savannah, Georgia.

\*

Maili Halme Brocke is Executive Chef and owner of Maili Productions, a Santa Barbara–based catering and event planning company specializing in celebrity events. Maili comes from a family of football players and has been cooking for gridiron events for decades.